FTM 2017

Companion Guide

to

Family Tree Maker®

Based on the original Companion Guide by

Tana L. Pedersen

2104-6-01

Contents

Introduction...xvii

What's New? xviii

Part 1: Getting Started 1

Chapter 1 **Installing Family Tree Maker**........................ 3

Installing Family Tree Maker 4

Registering the Software 4

Getting Help 5

    Onscreen Help 5

    Companion Guide 6

    Technical Support 7

    Feedback... 7

Chapter 2 **Family Tree Maker Basics**........................ 9

Opening and Closing Family Tree Maker 9

The Family Tree Maker Interface 9

    Toolbars 10

    Menus and Keyboard Shortcuts 10

Workspaces Overview 10

    The Plan Workspace 10

    The People Workspace.. 12

    The Places Workspace.. 18

    The Media Workspace 19

The Sources Workspace..20

The Publish Workspace 21

The Web Search Workspace....................................22

Chapter 3 Creating a Tree 23

Before You Begin 23

Creating a Tree..23

Entering Your Information from Scratch............23

Importing a Tree File..24

Downloading a Tree from Ancestry....................26

Creating a copy of an existing tree on another

computer 29

Choosing a Home Person.......................................30

Part 2: Building a Tree 33

Chapter 4 Entering Family Information 35

Entering Basic Information for an Individual 35

Adding a Spouse...37

Adding a Child to a Family..................................39

Adding Parents 40

Adding More Details 41

Adding a Fact...41

Copying and Pasting Facts....................................44

Adding a Note for an Individual 47

Adding Web Links for an Individual....................49

Colour Coding..50

Applying colour coding to a person in your tree 51

Removing colour coding..52

Working with Relationships.....................................53

Using the Combined Family View.........................53

Viewing an Individual's Family Relationships.....54

Adding Additional Spouses 55
Choosing a Type of Relationship for a Couple....57
Choosing a Status for a Couple's Relationship 58
Choosing a Relationship Between Parents and a
Child 58
Adding an Unrelated Individual 59
Viewing a Timeline 59
Creating Smart Stories™...60
Creating a Smart Story as a Media Item.............61
Creating a Smart Story as a Report......................62
Including a Short Biography..................................63
Including Facts 63
Including Sources..65
Including Notes 66
Including Images...66
Creating Timelines..67
Editing Smart Stories Text 67

Chapter 5   Documenting Your Research........................ 69
Understanding Sources and Source Citations 69
Creating Sources...71
Adding a Source for a Fact....................................71
Using Source Templates 72
Creating a Source Using the Basic Format 75
Creating Source Citations 77
Adding a New Source Citation 77
Attaching a Media Item to a Source Citation 81
Adding a Note to a Source Citation.....................82
Using Source Repositories..83
Managing Repositories...84

Chapter 6 Including Media Items.................................... 89

    Adding Media Items... 90

        Adding a Media Item for an Individual 90

        Scanning an Image into Your Tree......................... 91

        Changing the Display of an Image......................... 92

    Entering Details for a Media Item................................. 93

    Entering a Note About a Media Item............................ 94

    Adding a Portrait for an Individual 95

    Editing Photos with Photo Darkroom......................... 96

    Linking a Media Item to Multiple Individuals 98

    Managing Media Items 100

        Opening a Media Item from Family Tree Maker 100

        Changing a Media Item's File Name 100

        Arranging an Individual's Media Items............. 100

    Media Categories 102

        Creating a Category 102

        Assigning a Category to Multiple Items............. 102

    Creating a Slide Show 103

    Printing a Media Item... 106

Chapter 7 Using Maps 107

    Viewing a Map 107

        Moving Around a Map.. 110

        Using Streetside View... 112

        Finding Places of Interest.................................... 113

        Printing a Map... 114

    Viewing Locations in Groups 115

    Viewing People and Facts Linked to a Location 115

    Creating Migration Maps... 117

        Creating a Migration Map for an Individual..... 117

        Creating a Migration Map for a Family 118

Entering GPS Coordinates 119

Entering a Display Name for a Location 120

Chapter 8 Researching Your Tree Online 121

Ancestry Hints... 121

FamilySearch Hints 122

Viewing Ancestry and FamilySearch Hints....... 122

Searching Ancestry 124

Searching FamilySearch... 130

Adding Records to a Tree 130

Searching Online with Family Tree Maker 134

Copying Online Facts.. 135

Copying an Online Image 137

Copying Online Text to a Note 138

Archiving a Web Page.. 140

Managing Research Websites.................................... 141

Adding a Website to Your Favourites List.......... 141

Sorting Your Website Favourites 142

Part 3: Creating Charts, Reports, and Books.. 143

Chapter 9 Creating Family Tree Charts 145

Pedigree Charts.. 145

Standard Pedigree Charts.................................... 146

Vertical Pedigree Charts 146

Hourglass Charts 147

Standard Hourglass Charts 147

Horizontal Hourglass Charts.............................. 149

Descendant Charts 150

Bow Tie Charts 151

Family Tree Charts 151

Fan Charts 152

Extended Family Charts 152

Relationship Charts.................................. 153

Creating a Chart 154

Customising a Chart 154

   Choosing Facts to Include in a Chart.............. 154

   Changing a Chart's Title......................... 156

   Including Source Information with a Chart...... 157

   Adding Images to a Chart 157

   Changing the Header or Footer 162

   Changing Formatting for a Chart 163

Using Chart Templates.............................. 168

   Creating Your Own Template...................... 169

   Using a Custom Template 169

Saving Charts 170

   Saving a Specific Chart 170

   Saving a Chart as a File........................ 170

Printing a Chart 171

Large Chart Printing 171

Sharing a Chart..................................... 172

Chapter 10 Running Reports............................. 173

Genealogy Reports 173

   Ahnentafel Report............................... 173

   Descendant Report 174

Person Reports...................................... 175

   Custom Report 175

   Data Errors Report.............................. 175

   Individual Report 176

   LDS Ordinances Report 176

   LDS Ordinance Summary Report................... 177

   List of Individuals Report 177

Notes Report 178
Surname Report 178
Task List 179
Timeline Report 179
Relationship Reports 180
Family Group Sheet 180
Kinship Report 181
Marriage Report 181
Outline Ancestor Report 182
Outline Descendant Report 182
Parentage Report 183
Family View Report 183
Place Usage Report 184
Media Reports 184
Photo Album 184
Media Item Report 185
Media Usage Report 186
Source Reports 186
Bibliography 186
Documented Facts Report 187
Undocumented Facts Report 187
Source Usage Report 188
Calendars 188
Creating a Report 189
Customising a Report 189
Choosing Facts to Include in a Report 189
Choosing Individuals to Include in a Report 192
Changing a Report's Title 193
Adding a Background Image 193
Changing the Header or Footer 194
Changing Fonts 195

Saving Reports 196
    Saving the Settings for a Report 196
    Saving a Specific Report 196
    Saving a Report as a File 197
Printing a Report 198
Sharing a Report 199

Chapter 11 Creating a Family History Book 201
The Desktop Book-Building Tool 201
Starting a Family History Book 201
    Accessing a Saved Book 202
Setting Up a Book 202
Adding Content to a Book 203
    Adding Text 203
    Adding Images 206
    Adding a Chart or Report 208
    Adding a Placeholder 208
    Creating a Table of Contents 209
    Creating an Index of Individuals 210
Organising a Book 210
    Changing an Item's Settings 211
    Rearranging Book Items 212
    Deleting a Book Item 213
Printing a Book at Home 213
Exporting a Book 213

Part 4: Managing Your Trees 215
Chapter 12 Working with Trees 217
Managing Your Trees 217
    Opening a Tree 217
    Viewing Information About a Tree 218

Renaming a Tree...218

Deleting a Tree..219

Using Privacy Mode..219

Exporting a Tree File..220

Backing Up Tree Files 222

Backing Up a Tree File 223

Restoring a Tree from a Backup 224

Compressing a Tree File 225

Uploading a Tree to Ancestry....................................225

Uploading and Linking a Tree to Ancestry 226

Differences Between FTM and Ancestry Trees.228

Working with Linked Trees.......................................229

Setting Up Syncing..230

Syncing Trees Manually......................................233

Getting Sync Weather Reports 233

Resolving Conflicts Between Linked Trees........234

Unlinking Trees...236

Changing Privacy Settings 236

Inviting Others to View Your Tree.....................237

Chapter 13 Tools and Preferences 241

Using Family Tree Maker Tools................................241

Soundex Calculator...241

Relationship Calculator 242

Date Calculator 243

Name Converter 244

Find Individual Tool 244

Automatic Reference Numbers 245

Global Birth Order Tool.....................................246

Research To-Do List 247

Setting Up Preferences................................250
  General Preferences 250
  Name Preferences................................254
  Date Preferences.................................255
  Warning and Alert Preferences 256
Managing Facts......................................258
  Creating a Custom Fact.....................258
  Modifying a Predefined Fact 260
  Modifying a Fact Sentence................260
Managing Historical Events 261
Customising the Tree Tab Editing Panel 263
Entering User Information.......................264

Chapter 14 Family Tree Problem Solver....................... 265
Straightening Out Relationships 265
  Merging Duplicate Individuals...........265
  Removing an Individual from a Tree.................269
  Removing a Marriage 269
  Detaching a Child from the Wrong Parents......270
  Attaching a Child to a Father and Mother........271
Fixing Text Mistakes 272
  Global Spell Checker 272
  Find and Replace Tool.......................273
  Merging Duplicate Facts....................275
Running the Data Errors Report 276
Standardising Locations 277
  Identifying a Single Location..............277
  Identifying Multiple Locations...........279
Finding Missing Media Items 280
  Finding a Single Missing Media Item..................280
  Finding All Missing Media Items........281

Troubleshooting... 283

Glossary 293

Index 297

Introduction

Congratulations on selecting Family Tree Maker to discover and preserve your family's heritage. It's easy to use for those just starting to research their family history, but it's also powerful enough for the most serious genealogists. Use Family Tree Maker to store, display, and share any kind of family information—from names, marriages, and deaths to priceless family stories, pictures, and videos.

This guide is designed to help you learn to use Family Tree Maker quickly, leaving you more time to discover your family history. If you have never used a genealogy program before, you'll find that the features in Family Tree Maker make it possible to keep track of the most tangled of family trees.

This book is written with the novice computer user in mind. You'll read about many of the useful tools that the casual Family Tree Maker user never discovers, and you'll be taken on a hands-on trip through the Family Tree Maker application. Illustrations throughout let you check your progress as you master each new feature or concept. Even if you are familiar with computers, though, you may have only recently been introduced to Family Tree Maker or simply want to know what great features you have not yet discovered in the program. This book offers you a step-by-step tour of the program and all that you can accomplish with it.

Before you begin entering your family's information, make sure you look through the "Family Tree Maker Basics" chapter. It will show you the skills you need to navigate through Family Tree Maker and will introduce you to the software's interface.

What's New?

New features and enhancements in Family Tree Maker 2017 make it easier than ever to discover your family history, build your family tree, and share your unique heritage. Here are four of the most notable new features you will find as you explore Family Tree Maker 2017:

 FamilySearch Integration. Family Tree Maker users can now directly access online records of FamilySearch, the world's largest collection of genealogical and historical records, much like they already do with Ancestry. Users can search more than a billion names in FamilySearch's Family Tree database, get match suggestions (hints), and merge the results into their trees. See pages 122-132.

 FamilySync™. An upgrade from Ancestry's TreeSync® technology, FamilySync allows Family Tree Maker 2017 users to synchronise the trees on their computer with Ancestry trees, as well as to simply upload their trees to and download their trees from Ancestry. Those using both a desktop and laptop computer will appreciate the new ability to sync both to a single Ancestry tree online. See pages 229-237.

 Colour Coding. Providing the ability to mark up to eight colours at a time on a single person, colour coding helps users organise their records and gain helpful insights into their family's unique history. Together with sophisticated filter tools, colour coding allows users to uncover crossed family lines and identify relationships that might otherwise have never been discovered. See pages 50-52.

Photo Darkroom™. Photo Darkroom provides elegantly simple but powerful photo editing tools designed specifically for genealogists. The first set of tools, a photo repair suite, makes it possible to take old black-and-white photographs faded beyond recognition and, in just a few clicks, restore them to look almost like the day they were printed. See pages 96-97.

How the Guide Is Organised

As you read this book, you'll notice several features that provide you with useful information:

- Tips give you advice on the best ways to perform tasks.

- Notes offer you timely hints and explanations about how features work.

- Sidebars give you additional information on a variety of family history topics, such as using maps, that will enhance your ability to create a richer and more complete family tree.

- A glossary explains words you might not be familiar with, such as Family Tree Maker terms (family group view, Fastfields), and genealogy terms (GEDCOM, Ahnentafel).

If you still need help, a quick perusal of the Table of Contents should lead you straight to the task you are trying to perform; if not, have a look at the index in the back of the book.

Part One
Getting Started

Chapter 1: Installing Family Tree Maker.................. 3

Chapter 2: Family Tree Maker Basics...................... 9

Chapter 3: Creating a Tree..................................... 23

Chapter One
Installing Family Tree Maker

This chapter lists the system requirements for Family Tree Maker, shows you how to install the software, and gives a quick introduction to available help resources.

Recommended System Requirements

To use Family Tree Maker 2017, you'll need a computer that meets the specifications below. Bear in mind that the more family information you enter, the greater the amount of free hard disk space and available RAM you will need. If you have lots of images or videos, you'll need a substantial amount of hard disk space.

- macOS 10.9 or later, including 10.13 "High Sierra"
- Any Intel-based Mac capable of running macOS 10.9
- 2 GB of memory (4 GB recommended)
- 900 MB of free disk space
- 1280×800 display resolution
- DVD drive (only if installing from a DVD)
- USB port (only if installing from a USB flash drive)

All online features require Internet access. The user is responsible for their Internet Service Provider (ISP) account, all Internet access fees, and phone charges.

Installing Family Tree Maker

To use Family Tree Maker the application must be installed on your computer's hard disk; you cannot run it directly from the DVD or the USB drive. If you have an earlier version of Family Tree Maker installed on your computer, this new version will not copy over it. While the installation process will not harm your existing Family Tree Maker files, it's always a good idea to back up your tree files on an external storage device or using a cloud storage service.

1   Insert the Family Tree Maker DVD into your Mac's drive, or double-click the .dmg file that you have downloaded or that is located on your Family Tree Maker USB Drive.

2   In the window that appears, double-click the **Family Tree Maker 2017** icon to launch the application installer.

3   Follow the onscreen instructions to complete the installation.

Note: If you experience any difficulties, please see the "Troubleshooting" chapter on page 288.

Registering the Software

Before you create your first tree, take a minute or two to register the software. Registered users get discounts on new editions of Family Tree Maker and notifications of software updates.

When you open the application for the first time, the registration dialog opens automatically. If you choose not to register on the first run, but decide to do so some time later, choose **Register Family Tree Maker 2017** from the **Family Tree Maker 2017** menu, and then follow the onscreen instructions. Make sure your computer is connected to the Internet before you start.

Getting Help

Family Tree Maker has onscreen help, this companion guide, and online technical support. If you have questions about a feature or simply want to learn more about the application, refer to one of these Help resources.

Onscreen Help

Family Tree Maker has convenient onscreen help to give you information on performing tasks and answer questions about the software. You can search help by typing in a topic or phrase. You can also print the resulting explanation.

Opening the Help Viewer

On the **Help** menu, choose **Family Tree Maker 2017 Help**. Family Tree Maker displays the Help Viewer (fig. 1-1).

Figure 1-1. The table of contents for Family Tree Maker Help.

> **Help Tags**
>
> If you want to know the name of a button or find out what it's used for,
> hold the pointer over it for a second or two and a help tag will appear.

Searching in the Help Program

Searching is the quickest way to find the topic you're interested in.
In the search field, type the word, phrase, or topic you want to know
more about. Many useful pages can be found by entering keywords
like "searching," "sources," "reports," and "notes."

When the search results appear, select a topic to open it. You can
use the **Share** ⬆ button and pop-up menu to print the current
help page. Press the **Command** and "+" keys to enlarge the text and
illustrations and the **Command** and "-" keys to make them smaller.

Tip: In many areas of Family Tree Maker you can press
Command+F1 to immediately open a help topic for the area
you are working in, or you can click the Help ⑦ button on
windows that have one.

Navigating in the Help Program

The onscreen help makes use of links to take you to other related
topics. These links are easily identified by their blue, underlined
text. Simply click any link to go to a new topic. You can also use
these buttons on the toolbar to move around within help:

- **Back and Forward buttons**—Click the **Back** button to return to
  a previous help topic; click the **Forward** button to move forward
  through the help topics you've already opened.

Companion Guide

To view this *Companion Guide* as a PDF, choose **Companion Guide**
on the **Help** menu.

Technical Support

Family Tree Maker has an online support center where you can get assistance with technical problems and answers to customer service questions. You'll start by searching our knowledge base of easy-to-understand articles with tips and step-by-step instructions. If that doesn't provide what you need, you can fill out an online support request and have an option to get an answer by email or be connected right away to our Live Chat service which is available 24 hours a day, 7 days a week. Choose **Family Tree Maker Tech Support** from the **Help** menu to get started.

Feedback

We'd love to hear from you with comments, questions or suggestions. Please visit the Family Tree Maker product page online. Choose **Provide Family Tree Maker Feedback** from the **Family Tree Maker 2017** application menu or go to www.familytreemaker.com, and then use one of the feedback options available there.

Chapter Two
Family Tree Maker Basics

Family Tree Maker makes it easy—and enjoyable—for anyone to discover their family history and gather it in one convenient location. And whether you're interested in printing family charts to share at a reunion or looking for an easy way to store your family facts, photos, and records, Family Tree Maker is the program to help you do it all.

This chapter gives you the basic skills and knowledge you need to launch the program and navigate around the software. Let's get started.

Opening and Closing Family Tree Maker

To open the application, click the **Family Tree Maker 2017** icon in the Dock or locate the software in the Applications folder and double-click the **Family Tree Maker 2017** icon.

To close the application, choose **Family Tree Maker 2017 > Quit Family Tree Maker**. There's no need to save your tree—Family Tree Maker automatically saves changes as you make them.

The Family Tree Maker Interface

To use any application effectively, the first step is to understand its unique interface and tools. You'll immediately recognise many common features in Family Tree Maker. However, there are some unique toolbars, menus, and dialogs you'll want to learn how to use and navigate.

Toolbars

The main toolbar in Family Tree Maker (fig. 2-1) is located at the top of the application below the menu bar. It provides quick navigation to various workspaces—groupings of the most important features in the application. On the far left of the toolbar, you'll find the Select Tree pop-up menu that lets you switch between trees.

Figure 2-1. The main toolbar.

Menus and Keyboard Shortcuts

Family Tree Maker menus work like in any other computer application. Simply choose a menu to display its commands; then, choose the command you want. Some menu commands have keyboard shortcuts that allow you to access features without using a mouse or trackpad.

Workspaces Overview

Family Tree Maker groups important features together in work-spaces. Each workspace has a slightly different appearance and purpose, but generally, they all contain the same elements, such as toolbars and tabs.

The Plan Workspace

The Plan workspace is the "control centre" where you manage your family trees. On the New Tree tab you can start a new tree, import an existing tree file, or download a tree from Ancestry.

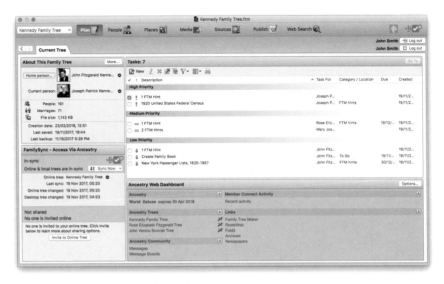

Figure 2-2. The Current Tree tab on the Plan workspace.

The Current Tree tab on the Plan workspace (fig. 2-2) lets you view details about your tree, manage your research to-do list, and, if you've linked your FTM tree to an Ancestry tree, you can also manage how the trees are synced.

The Current Tree tab also contains the Ancestry Web Dashboard where you can see the status of your Ancestry subscription if you have one (double-click it to access your Ancestry account), open your Ancestry trees, and view your Member Connect activity.

What Is Member Connect on Ancestry?

Member Connect helps you stay in touch with others who are researching your ancestors. Ancestry scans public Ancestry trees and notifies you when there's activity around records you've saved or commented on.

The People Workspace

The People workspace is where you enter information about individuals and families in your tree—and where you will spend most of your time in Family Tree Maker.

The Tree tab (fig. 2-3) provides a comprehensive view of your family. You can see several generations of your family at once and easily navigate to each person in your tree. Because you will use this tab often, its various sections will be explained in detail.

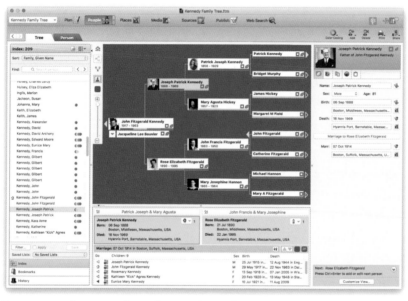

Figure 2-3. The Tree tab on the People workspace.

The Index

The Index (fig. 2-4) lists all the individuals in your tree and is one of the easiest ways to locate the person you want to focus on. To view information for a specific individual, click his or her name in the Index. If you can't see the person you want, use the scroll bar to move up and down the list, or type a name in the Find field to jump to a particular person.

The house icon indicates the individual who is the current home person in the tree. (You'll learn more about the home person in chapter 3.)

To make it easier to locate individuals, you can change how the Index sorts names using the **Sort** pop-up menu. You can display birth, marriage, or death dates as well by clicking the **Show additional data** button.

You can also limit the Index so it displays only certain individuals; click the **Filter** button and select a specific family line, an individual's descendants, or a group of your choice. Click the **Bookmarks** button to see a list of individuals you have specifically bookmarked, or click the **History** button to see the individuals you have added or edited recently.

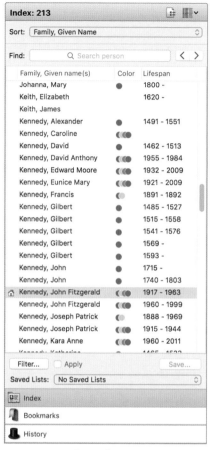

Figure 2-4. The Index.

Saving and Opening Filtered Lists of People

When you have applied a filter, you may want to retain the list of people that it produced so that you can return to it whenever you need. You can save the list by clicking the **Save** button at the bottom of the Index. In the dialog that appears, give the list a name and click **Save**. You can also choose a colour. This colour will be assigned to all the people in the list and displayed next to their names in the Index and on their thumbnails in the tree viewer, exactly as colours assigned with colour coding are. For more information about colour coding, see the "Colour Coding" section on page 50.

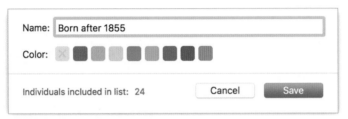

Figure 2-5. The Save List dialog.

When you save your list, it appears in the **Saved Lists** pop-up menu below the **Save** button. To open a saved list, click the pop-up menu and choose the list you want.

Managing Saved Lists

- To manage lists, choose **Manage Lists** from the **Saved Lists** pop-up menu.

- To add a new list, either save an existing one (see "Saving and Opening Filtered Lists of People" above) or click the "plus" button in the **Manage Lists** dialog. The **Filter Individuals** dialog appears. Set up a filter to produce the list you need, and then click **Apply**. In the dialog that appears, give the list a name and, optionally, choose a colour, and then click **OK**.

- To delete an existing list, select its name in the **Manage Lists** dialog, and then click the "minus" button.

- To change a list's name or colour, select the list in the **Manage Lists** dialog, and then edit the name in the **Name** field or click a different color.

The Tree Viewer

The tree viewer (fig. 2-6) helps you navigate through your family tree as well as add new individuals.

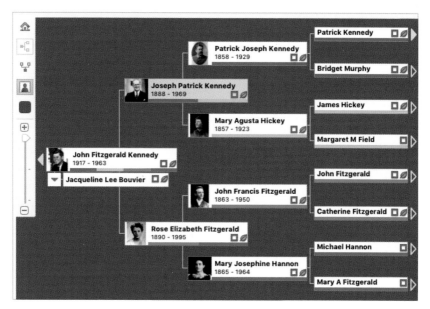

Figure 2-6. The pedigree view in the tree viewer.

These buttons will help you use the tree viewer:

 Go to home person. Makes the home person the primary individual or focus of the tree.

 Pedigree view. Shows a pedigree view of your tree. The primary individual or focus of the tree is on the left, with ancestors branching out to the right.

 Family view. Shows a family view of your tree. The primary individual is at the base of the tree, with ancestors branching above—paternal on the left and maternal on the right.

 Include pictures. Displays portraits and lifespans for each individual in the pedigree view.

Re-center on selected person. Adjusts the tree to focus on the currently selected person in the family view.

 Change background color. Lets you choose the tree viewer's background colour.

The Editing Panel

The editing panel (fig. 2-7) is where you'll enter basic information about an individual, such as birth, marriage, and death dates and places. At the top you'll find a portrait of an individual (if you've added one) and how he or she is related to the home person. Toolbar buttons under the portrait let you display media items, notes, Web links, and tasks associated with the individual.

Figure 2-7. The editing panel.

The Family Group View

The family group view (fig. 2-8) lets you view an individual's spouse and children.

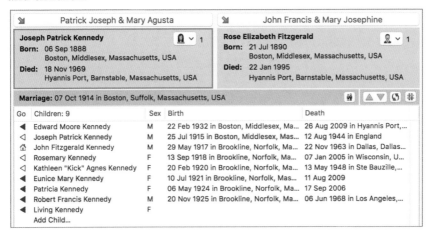

Figure 2-8. The family group view on the People workspace.

Click the "parents" button above the individual to display his or her parents and siblings. The toolbar buttons let you edit the couple's marriage fact, change the display order of their children, and view blended families.

The Person Tab

The Person tab on the People workspace (fig. 2-9) lets you add facts, media items, Web links, and notes for an individual. You can also view a timeline for an individual and their relationships to other family members.

Figure 2-9. The Person tab on the People workspace.

The Places Workspace

The Places workspace (fig. 2-10) helps you view the locations you've entered for events—and gives you the opportunity to view online maps of them. The Places panel on the left shows every location you've entered in your tree. When you select a place, it will be displayed in the map at the centre of the workspace. The details panel on the right side shows the individuals who have life events associated with the location.

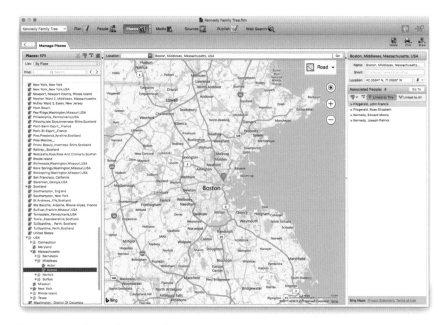

Figure 2-10. The Places workspace.

The Media Workspace

The Media workspace acts as a storage space for your photos, audio recordings, videos, family documents, and historical records. On the Media Collection tab (fig. 2-11) you can view thumbnails of your media items and enter information about them. On the Media Detail tab you can add notes for an item and link it to individuals and source citations.

Figure 2-11. The Collection tab on the Media workspace.

The Sources Workspace

The Sources workspace (fig. 2-12) organises your sources and source citations. The Source Groups panel on the left lets you sort sources by person, title, and repository; the sources display area shows which citations have been entered for a specific source. Tabs at the bottom of the window show the individuals linked to a source citation, related notes, and media items. In the editing panel, you can enter or update specific source citations.

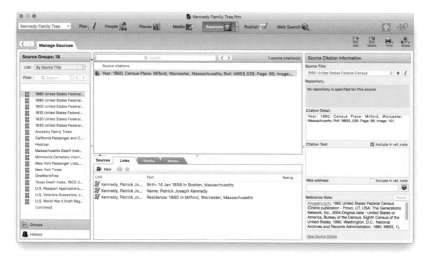

Figure 2-12. The Sources workspace.

The Publish Workspace

The Publish workspace offers a variety of charts and reports that you can view, print, and share. You can also create family history books. The Publish Collection tab (fig. 2-13) shows the types of charts and reports that are available and gives an explanation of each.

On the Publish Detail tab you can customise a chart or report using the editing panel and preview your changes.

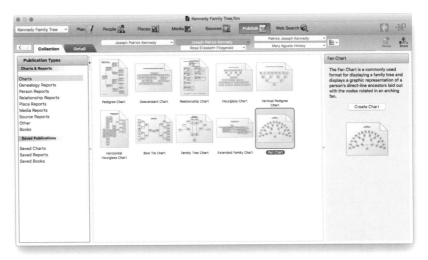

Figure 2-13. The Collection tab on the Publish workspace.

The Web Search Workspace

The Web Search workspace (fig. 2-14) lets you search billions of records on Ancestry and FamilySearch to find more information about your relatives—all without leaving Family Tree Maker. You can also search other websites and easily download discoveries into your tree.

Figure 2-14. The Web Search workspace.

Chapter Three
Creating a Tree

Before You Begin

This chapter assumes that you have installed Family Tree Maker and read chapters 1 and 2. Once you've got to know a few of the basic Family Tree Maker features, you're ready to create your first tree. Make sure you have some family information close at hand or have a file, such as a GEDCOM or Ancestry tree, to use.

Creating a Tree

A tree is where you gather and enter your family facts and details. If you've received a family history file from another family member or researcher, you can import the file, creating a new tree. Then you can begin adding your own information. You can also create a tree by entering a few quick facts about yourself or by downloading a tree you've created on Ancestry. Yet another way is to create a backup of an existing tree you have in Family Tree Maker 2017 on another computer and move it to the current computer. This allows you to keep two FTM trees (or more if you wish) and a linked Ancestry tree in sync. See "Working with Linked Trees" on page 229.

Entering Your Information from Scratch

If this is your first time creating a family tree, you'll want to use this option. Enter a few facts about yourself and your parents, and you're on your way.

1   Choose **File** > **New**. The New Tree tab opens.

2   Select **Enter What You Know**.

3   Type your name and choose your gender. You can also type your birth date and place and your parents' names.

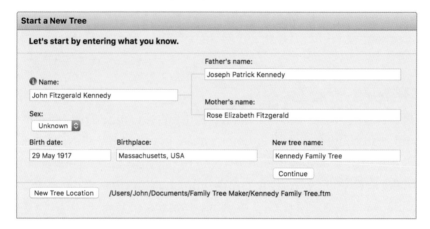

4   Type a name for the tree in the **New tree name** field.

5   By default, your tree will be saved to a Family Tree Maker folder in the Documents folder on your hard disk. To save the tree to another folder, click **New Tree Location**.

6   Click **Continue**. The tree opens on the People workspace, where you can start entering your family information.

Importing a Tree File

If you've already created a tree file or received one from a family member, you can import it. Tree files from Family Tree Maker for Mac (.ftm, .ftmm, and .ftmd), files from previous versions of Family Tree Maker for Windows (.ftw, .ftm, and .fbk), and GEDCOMs (GEnealogical Data COMmunications format) are all compatible.

1 If you haven't already, copy the tree file you want to import to your computer.

2 Choose **File** > **New**. The New Tree tab opens.

3 Select **Import an Existing Tree**.

4 Click **Choose** to locate the tree file you want to import. If you are importing a Family Tree Maker file, a dialog will appear for you to save a copy of it with a different name, and then the tree will open on the People workspace. If you are importing a GEDCOM file, follow the steps below.

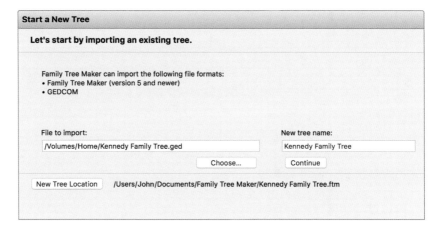

5 By default, your tree file will be saved to a Family Tree Maker folder in the Documents folder on your hard disk. To save the tree file to another folder, click **New Tree Location**.

6 If necessary, change the file's name in the **New tree name** field.

7 Click **Continue**. You'll see a message, which shows statistics for the new tree, including the number of individuals, families, and sources that were imported.

8 Click **Close**. The tree opens on the People workspace, where you can start entering your family information.

How Many Trees Should You Create?

When most beginners create a family tree, their first question is, "Should I create one large, all-inclusive tree or several small trees, one for each family?" The truth is, there is no right answer.

The advantages to having one large tree are pretty clear. One computer file is easier to keep track of—one file to enter information in, one file to back up, one file to share. Also, you won't have to duplicate your efforts by entering some facts, sources, and media items in several trees.

Multiple trees can be useful too. The more trees you have, the smaller the tree files will typically be. If you have concerns about your computer's performance or have storage issues, smaller files might work best. Smaller tree files also make it easier to collaborate with other family members; you can send them only the family lines they're interested in.

Whichever way you organise your trees initially, don't feel like you're stuck with a permanent decision. The flexible nature of Family Tree Maker means you can merge files anytime; you can even export parts of your tree to create a brand new tree.

Downloading a Tree from Ancestry

If you've created a tree on Ancestry, you don't need to start over in Family Tree Maker; you can download the tree to your computer. It will include all the facts, sources, and images you have attached to individuals.

Note: To download an Ancestry tree, you must be the tree's owner; you can't download trees you've been invited to view or edit.

Downloading and Linking a Tree in Family Tree Maker

When you download a tree from Ancestry, you create a link between your online Ancestry tree and its corresponding tree on your computer. This means that additions, deletions, or edits you make in your Family Tree Maker tree will be duplicated in your Ancestry tree (and vice versa) when you sync. (For more information, see "Differences Between FTM and Ancestry Trees" on page 228 and "Working with Linked Trees" on page 229.)

> Note: When you download your Ancestry tree, a new FTM tree will be created and linked to your Ancestry tree. You can merge the new FTM tree with another FTM tree later if you wish, but not during the download.

1   Make sure you are logged in to your Ancestry account (if necessary click the **Log In** button).

2   Choose **File** > **New**. The New Tree tab opens.

3   Select **Download a Tree from Ancestry**. A list of your trees on Ancestry appears.

4   Select the tree that you want to download. A summary of the tree status appears to the right of the list of the trees.

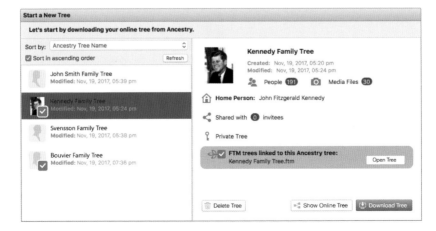

5   Click the **Download Tree** button.

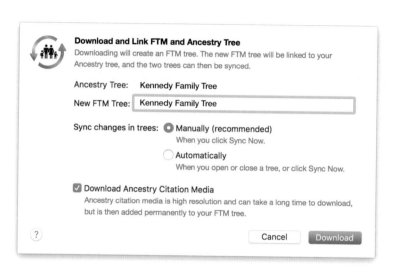

6   To change the name of the tree, type the new name in the **New FTM Tree** field.

7   Choose whether your Ancestry and FTM trees will be synced manually or automatically. (For help see "Setting Up Syncing" on page 230.)

8   Select the **Download Ancestry Citation Media** checkbox to also download Ancestry record images attached to your tree.

    Note: Ancestry Citation Media will not be downloaded unless you have a current Ancestry subscription. You can check your subscription status in the Web Dashboard. See page 11.

9   Click **Download**. When the tree has been downloaded successfully, click **Close**.

Creating a copy of an existing tree on another computer

If you already have a tree on Ancestry and on one of your computers, you can move a copy of it to a different computer on which Family Tree Maker 2017 is installed and keep all of the trees in sync. To do so, create a full backup of your existing FTM tree, copy it to your other computer using a flash drive, and then restore the tree there.

On the computer with the tree that you want to copy, do this:

1 In Family Tree Maker, open the tree that you want to copy.

2 Sync your tree file with the Ancestry tree.

3 Choose **File > Backup**.

4 Select the checkboxes to include media files from the tree's media folder, historical events, and web favourites in the backup.

5 Make sure that the **Allow restored file to resume syncing** checkbox is selected.

6 Choose a location on your computer to save the backup file.
   Note: If backing up directly to a flash drive fails and you get an error message, try to back up to your computer and then copy the backup file to your flash drive.

7 Click **Backup**.

Now copy the backup file onto your flash drive and then copy it from the flash drive onto the other computer.

On the computer to which you have moved the backup file, do this:

1 Choose **File > Restore**.

2 Select the backup file and click **Open**.

3   Choose the location where you want Family Tree Maker to store your copied tree.

4   Click **Save**.

5   In the dialog that appears, make sure that the **Allow restored file to resume syncing** checkbox is selected, and then click **Restore**.

Choosing a Home Person

Each tree has a home person. By default, this is the first person you enter in a tree. If you're creating a tree based on your family, the home person is most likely to be you. However, the home person can be anyone in your tree.

Occasionally, you may want to switch the home person. For example, if you're working on a specific family line, you may want to make someone in that ancestral line the home person.

Changing the Home Person on the Plan Workspace

1   Click the **Plan** button on the main toolbar. At the top of the Current Tree tab, you'll see the current home person.

2   Click the **Home person** button. The Index of Individuals opens.

3   Select the individual you want to be the home person and click **OK**. This individual becomes the new home person.

Changing the Home Person on the People Workspace

1   Click the **People** button on the main toolbar; then click the **Tree** tab.

2   Find the appropriate person in the family group view or Index; then Control-click and choose **Set As Home Person** from the shortcut menu.

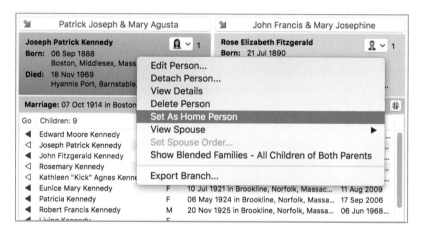

Part Two
Building a Tree

Chapter 4: Entering Family Information 35

Chapter 5: Documenting Your Research 69

Chapter 6: Including Media Items 89

Chapter 7: Using Maps 107

Chapter 8: Researching Your Tree Online 121

Chapter Four
Entering Family Information

Much of your time using Family Tree Maker will be spent entering the names, dates, and events that you've uncovered about your family. The simplest way to build your tree is to begin with what you already know—basic details about yourself, your spouse, your children, and your parents. As your tree grows, your focus can turn to ancestral lines, such as your grandparents and great-grandparents.

When you've entered basic birth, marriage, and death information for your family, you can expand your tree by adding marriage details, immigration stories, medical histories, and more.

Entering Basic Information for an Individual

You can enter facts about an individual (such as birth and death dates) on the Tree tab in the People workspace.

1 Click the **People** button on the main toolbar to open the People workspace.

2 Select an individual in the tree viewer or Index. The person's name and gender will be displayed in the editing panel.

3 In the editing panel, type a date in the **Birth** field.

4 Type the location where the individual was born in the **Birth Place** field.

Tip: As you type a place name, you'll notice that a list of possible matches appears. To use a suggested location, select it. To ignore the suggestion, continue typing.

5   If you know an individual's death date and place, enter this too. You can now continue by adding marriage facts, entering additional family members, entering facts for the individual, or adding photographs.

Entering Dates

Family Tree Maker automatically converts dates to the standard format used by genealogists: day, month, year. For example, 26 Sept 1961. If the application can't interpret the date you entered, a message asks for clarification. Simply retype the date in the standard format.

If you don't know the date of an event, you can leave the Date field blank or type "Unknown". If you have an approximate date, you can indicate this by typing "About 1920" or "Abt. 1920".

Entering Locations

Recording locations accurately and completely is an important part of your family history. Generally, you'll enter a location from the smallest to largest division. For example, for the United Kingdom, you would enter city or town or village, parish or district, province or county, country (Witton, Aston, Warwickshire, England). For the United States, you would enter city or town, county, state, country (Haddam, Washington, Kansas, United States).

- To help you enter locations quickly and consistently, Family Tree Maker has a locations database that includes more than 3 million place names. When you type a location, Family Tree Maker checks the name against the database and suggests possible matches. You can select a location from the list or add your own place name.

- Click the **Go to Place** ![icon] icon next to a place field to open the Places workspace and centre the map on the corresponding location.

Adding a Spouse

1   Click **Add Spouse** in the family group view. In the field that appears, type the spouse's name (first, middle, and last). Don't forget to use maiden names for women.

2 Choose a gender from the pop-up menu and click **Done**. The spouse is now the focus of the tree viewer and editing panel.

3 Enter any basic facts (such as birth and death) you have for the new spouse.

Entering Details About a Relationship

After you've added a spouse for an individual, you'll want to include any additional information you have about the couple. You can enter shared facts (such as marriage or divorce), notes, and media items (such as wedding photos).

1 Go to the **Tree** tab on the People workspace and select the appropriate individual.

2 To add a marriage date and place, type the information in the appropriate fields.

3 To enter more information for the couple, click the **Marriage to** button; then click a tab to enter facts, notes, or media items.

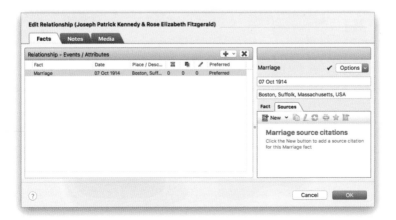

Entering Names

To keep names in your tree consistent, you'll want to follow these guidelines:

- Make sure you use a woman's maiden name (her last name, or surname, before she was married). This helps you trace her family and keeps you from confusing her with other people in your tree.

- You may have last names (surnames) that are not a single word. You'll need to identify these names with backslashes (\); otherwise, Family Tree Maker will read only the last word as the surname. Here are some examples:

    George \de la Vergne\   Teresa \Garcia Ramirez\

Adding a Child to a Family

1   In the family group view, click **Add Child**. Then type the child's name (first, middle, and last) and click **Done**.

Tip: Family Tree Maker assumes that a child has the same last name as the father and automatically fills it in for you. You can ignore the suggested name by typing over it.

2   In the editing panel, select a gender and type any birth and
    death information you have for the child.

Changing the Sort Order of Children

You can change the order in which children appear in the family
group view. For example, your direct ancestor can be displayed at
the top of the list regardless of his or her birth order, or you can
display all children by birth order. You can change the sort order of
children only when the **Show blended families** option is turned off.

1   Go to the **Tree** tab on the People workspace and select the
    appropriate family.

2   Select a child in the family group view.

3   Do one of the following:

    •   Click the **Move child up** ▲ and **Move child down** ▼
        buttons to move a child to a specific place in the order.

    •   Click the **Sort children** button to display the children
        in their birth order. Choose whether you want to sort this
        family only or all children in your tree. Then click **OK**.

Adding Parents

When you've added your spouse and children to your tree, you'll
want to continue with your parents, grandparents, great-grandparents, and so on.

1   Go to the **Tree** tab on the People workspace. In the Index or
    tree viewer, select the individual you want to add a father or
    mother to.

2   Click **Add Father** or **Add Mother** in the tree viewer.

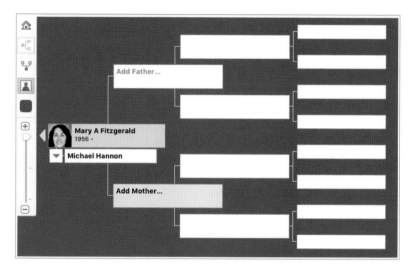

3   Type the parent's name (first, middle, and last) and click **Done**.
    Don't forget to use maiden names for women.

4   In the editing panel, select a gender and type any birth and
    death information you have for the individual.

Adding More Details

So far, you've only entered basic facts for a person. Now you can
add more details and notes.

Adding a Fact

In addition to birth and death events, you can add facts such as
christening, immigration, and occupations.

Note: You'll want to record the source of each fact. A source is where you discovered the information, such as a book or historical record. For more information, see Chapter 5.

1   Go to the **Tree** tab on the People workspace and select the appropriate individual. Then click the **Person** tab.

2   Click the **Facts** button to open the Individual & Shared Facts pane, which shows the facts you've already entered for the individual.

3   Click the **Add Fact** ✚ ⌄ button in the top-right corner of the Individual & Shared Facts pane. The Add Fact dialog opens.

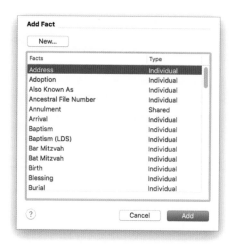

4   Select a fact in the list and click **Add**.

Tip: You can add your own fact types (for example, university graduation) by clicking the **New** button.

Notice that the editing panel on the right side of the workspace displays the appropriate fields for the fact.

5   Fill in the **Date**, **Place**, **Description**, and **Value** fields as necessary.

Note: Don't forget to add a source for each fact. For instructions, see "Creating Sources" on page 71.

Common Facts

In addition to birth, marriage, and death events, here are some facts you will probably encounter as you record your family history:

- **Address.** Addresses can be useful for keeping contact information for living relatives or for recording where an ancestor lived.

- **Also Known As.** Use this fact if an individual was known by a nickname rather than his or her given name.

- **Baptism and Christening.** Birth records are not always available, so these records become useful because they may be the earliest available information you can find for an ancestor.

- **Burial.** If you can't find a death record for an individual, but you have a burial record, you can use this information to estimate a person's death date.

- **Cause of Death/Medical Condition.** Knowing your family's health history may help you prevent and treat illnesses that run in families. You can record an individual's cause of death or enter details you know about an individual's medical history, from long-term illness to simple things such as "suffers from hay fever."

- **Emigration/Immigration.** Emigration and immigration records are the first step in finding ancestors who came from overseas in their homeland. Use these facts to record dates, ports of departure and arrival, and even ship names.

- **Physical Description.** Although not necessarily beneficial to your research, a physical description of an ancestor can be a fascinating addition to any family history.

- **Title.** If an individual has a title, such as Captain, you can use it to tell the difference between the individual and others with the same or similar names.

Copying and Pasting Facts

You can copy a fact from one person and paste it into the facts for another person. This is useful if several family members share the same fact (such as residence), and you don't want to create a new fact for each person.

1   Go to the **Tree** tab on the People workspace and select the appropriate individual. Then click the **Person** tab.

2   Click the **Facts** button.

3   Control-click the fact you want to copy and choose **Copy** from the shortcut menu.

4   Use the mini pedigree tree above the workspace to go the person you want to add the fact to.

5   Control-click the Individual & Shared Facts pane and choose **Paste**. A list of immediate family members appears.

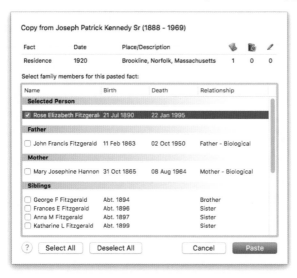

6   Select the checkbox next to each person you want to add the fact to; then click **Paste**.

Adding Alternate Facts

As you add facts, you may discover conflicting information about the same life event, such as two birth dates. When you have multiple facts for the same event, one fact will be "preferred", and the others will be "alternates" (that is, alternative facts).

> Note: An alternate fact doesn't have to include conflicting information. For example, you may have three Address facts for an individual, all of which are correct.

Choosing a Preferred Fact

When you enter multiple facts for the same life event, you'll have to choose which fact is preferred. Typically, this is the fact that is the most accurate or complete. Preferred facts are shown by default in the editing panel, charts, and reports.

1   Go to the **Tree** tab on the People workspace and select the appropriate individual. Then click the **Person** tab.

2   Select the fact you want to be preferred.

3   In the editing panel, click the **Options** button and choose **Preferred** from the pop-up menu.

The Preferred column in the Individual & Shared Facts pane now shows the fact as preferred.

Tip: You can also set a preferred fact by Control-clicking the fact and choosing **Set As Preferred** from the shortcut menu.

Making a Fact Private

You may enter facts that you don't want to share with other family members or researchers. If you make a fact private, you can choose whether or not to include it in reports and when you export a tree.

1   Go to the **Tree** tab on the People workspace and select the appropriate individual. Then click the **Person** tab.

2   Click **Facts**; then select the fact you want to make private.

3   In the editing panel, click the **Options** button and choose **Mark as Private** from the pop-up menu.

A lock icon 🔒 will appear next to the private fact in the Individual & Shared Facts pane.

Adding a Note for an Individual

You may have family stories, legends, or research resources that you want to refer to occasionally. Family Tree Maker lets you enter this type of information in notes—up to 1MB of space, or about 200 printed pages, per note.

> Tip: If you are entering notes from another document on your computer, you can "copy and paste" so you don't have to retype existing text.

Entering a Personal Note

Personal notes may be as simple as a physical description or as lengthy as a transcript of an interview with your grandmother.

> Note: You should *not* record source information on the Notes tab; if you do, the information won't be included in source reports.

1 Go to the **Tree** tab on the People workspace and select the appropriate individual. Then click the **Person** tab.

2 Click the **Notes** tab at the bottom of the **Person** tab. Then click the **Person note** button in the notes toolbar.

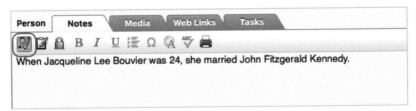

3 Place the insertion point in the notes area and type your text.

Entering a Research Note

Sometimes a record or family story will give you clues that can help you learn more about your family. You can create research notes to remind you of the next steps you want to take.

1 Go to the **Tree** tab on the People workspace and select the appropriate individual. Then click the **Person** tab.

2 Click the **Notes** tab at the bottom of the Person tab. Then click the **Research note** ![icon] button in the Notes toolbar.

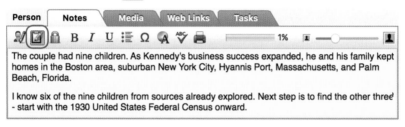

3 Place the insertion point in the notes area and type your text.

Changing a Note's Display Size

You can resize your notes to make the text larger and easier to read or make the text smaller to fit more words on the tab. Simply drag the slider on the right side of the Notes toolbar (fig. 4-1). This only changes how the note is displayed; it does not change how it will be printed.

Figure 4-1. A slider on the Notes tab lets you resize the text.

Making a Note Private

You may have information about a relative that you don't want to share with other researchers. If you make a note private, you can choose whether or not to include it in reports and when you export a tree.

After entering a note, click the **Mark as Private** 🔒 button in the notes toolbar. You can tell the note has been marked as private because the lock icon will have a border around it.

Figure 4-2. The Mark as Private button in its two states.

Printing a Note

To print a note, click the printer button on the Notes toolbar. Select your printing options and click **Print**.

Tip: You can also create a report of any notes you've entered in your tree. Go to the Publish workspace and select **Person Reports**. Then double-click **Notes Report**.

Adding Web Links for an Individual

If you want to keep track of a website you have found about an ancestor or an interesting collection of online maps, you can create a Web link so you can easily access it again.

1   Go to the **Tree** tab on the People workspace and select the appropriate individual. Then click the **Person** tab.

2   Click the **Web Links** tab at the bottom of the **Person** tab. Then click the **New** button in the toolbar.

3   Enter the address for the website.

Note: Family Tree Maker Web links cannot be synced with Web links in your Ancestry tree at present. See "Differences between FTM and Ancestry Trees" on page 228.

4   Enter a name for the link.

5   Click **Add**.

Colour Coding

When you are working on a large tree, it can sometimes be difficult to trace family lines through the generations without creating a relationship report. To help you see lineages at a glance, Family Tree Maker allows you to use colour coding to mark all the direct-line ancestors and descendants of any given person. The colouring scheme is based on the classic four-colour system created by Mary E. V. Hill, but has been further extended to give you more colouring options.

You can highlight a selected person's descendants with one colour and his or her ancestors with another. Or, for ancestors, you can use a four-colour system to apply different colours to four different lineages: the paternal father's line, the paternal mother's line, the maternal father's line, and the maternal mother's line.

You can apply one of the four-colour choices to one parent, and another four-colour palette to another parent, producing the full eight colours in the tree viewer. You can also mark any individual with a colour. This can be useful to highlight a person for whom additional research is needed, for example, or conversely, a person whose information you consider to be complete.

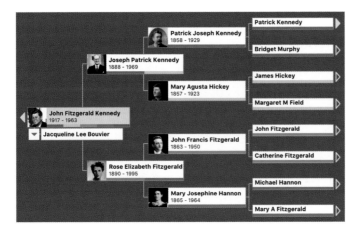

Applying colour coding to a person in your tree

1 Go to the **Tree** tab on the **People** workspace.

2 Select the person you want to highlight or whose ancestors and descendants you want to highlight.

3 Click the **Color Coding** button above the editing panel.

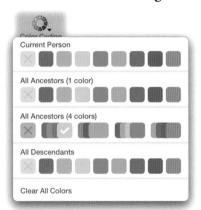

4 Click a colour or a colour group for the type of individuals to whom you want to apply colour coding: **Current Person, All Ancestors (1 color), All Ancestors (4 colors),** or **All Descendants.**

Coloured bars now appear on all the relevant person thumbnails in the tree viewer. Coloured dots are also shown next to the corresponding names in the Index and in the lists of people on the Places, Media, and Sources workspaces.

If you have applied colour coding for several selected individuals in your tree, there may be some people who belong to more than one family line—in this case all the corresponding colours will be displayed on those individuals' thumbnails. To find out why a person is marked with a particular colour, hold the pointer over the coloured bar on his or her thumbnail. A help tag will appear with the explanation.

Another great way to use colour coding is as an attribute of a certain criterion - in other words, an additional, at-a-glance filter. For example, you can create a filter of all persons who served in the military, or lived in a certain location, then assign a colour to that attribute and save your filter. This allows you to easily see the persons that satisfy the criterion both in the Index panel, and in the tree viewer. To learn more about creating filters see "The Index" on page 12.

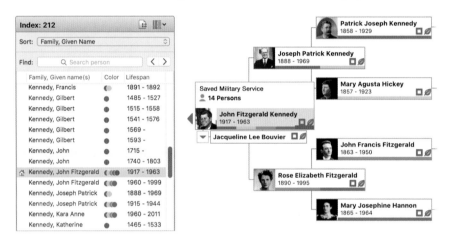

Removing colour coding for an individual or individual's lineage

1   On the **Tree** tab of the **People** workspace, select a person to whom colour coding has been applied.

2   Click the **Color Coding** button above the editing panel.

3   Click the **No Color** ✕ button for the color coding that you want to remove.

To remove all color coding from your tree, click the **Color Coding** button above the editing panel, and then click **Clear All Colors**.

Working with Relationships

As you dig deeper into your family history you will discover individuals who marry multiple times, divorces, adoptions, and other special situations. Family Tree Maker can handle all different types of relationships.

Using the Combined Family View

The family group view on the People workspace displays a couple and their mutual children. You can change this view so it displays all children associated with the couple, including children from previous marriages and relationships.

Note: When you display a "blended family" in the family group view, you cannot change the sort order of the children; they will be listed chronologically according to birth date.

1   Go to the **Tree** tab on the People workspace and select the appropriate family.

2   Click the **Show blended families** 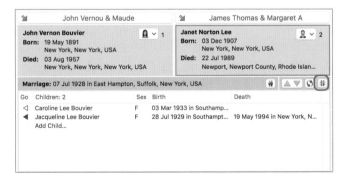 button in the family group view.

The combined family group view now displays all the children of both individuals. An icon to the left of the child's name

indicates whether he or she is the child of the father, the
mother, or both parents.

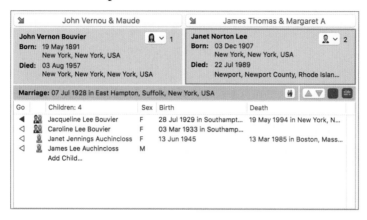

3 To return to the traditional family group view, simply click the
Show blended families button again.

Viewing an Individual's Family Relationships

You can see all the members of an individual's family at a glance—
spouses, children, parents, and siblings.

1 Select the appropriate individual and go to the **Person** tab on
the People workspace.

2 Click **Relationships** to display the Relationships pane, which
shows how the individual is related to others in the tree.

Adding Additional Spouses

If an individual in your family has been married more than once, you'll want to enter all additional spouses.

1 Go to the **Tree** tab on the People workspace and select the appropriate individual.

2 In the family group view, click the **Choose spouse** 🔲 button next to the individual. From the pop-up menu, you can view the existing spouse or add a new spouse.

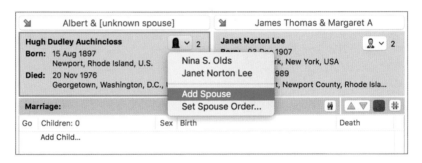

3 Choose **Add Spouse**.

4 Type the name of the new spouse and click **Add**. Family Tree Maker displays a new family group view—this time with the new spouse.

5 To view the first spouse again, click the **Choose spouse** button and choose his or her name from the pop-up menu.

Choosing a Preferred Spouse

If you enter more than one spouse for an individual, you need to indicate who is the preferred spouse. (This is usually the spouse whose children are in your direct family line.) The preferred spouse

will be the default spouse displayed in the family group view, tree
viewer, and charts and reports.

1 Go to the **Tree** tab on the People workspace and select the
appropriate individual.

2 Click the **Person** tab and then click the **Relationships** button.
You should see two or more names listed under the Spouses
heading.

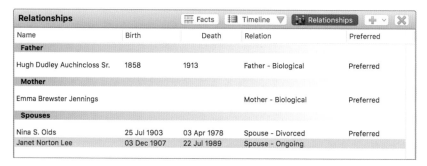

3 Select the individual you want to be the preferred spouse. Then,
in the editing panel, select the **Preferred spouse** checkbox.

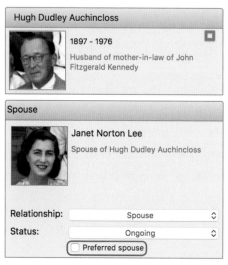

Switching Between Multiple Spouses

Family Tree Maker displays a person's preferred spouse by default, but you can switch to other spouses when necessary.

1   Go to the **Tree** tab on the People workspace and select the appropriate individual.

2   In the family group view, click the **Choose spouse** button next to the individual. From the pop-up menu, choose the spouse you want to view.

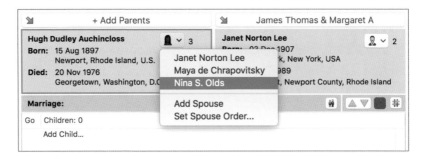

Choosing a Type of Relationship for a Couple

You can choose what type of relationship a couple has (e.g., partner, friend, spouse).

1   Go to the **Tree** tab on the People workspace and select the appropriate couple.

2   Click the **Person** tab; then click **Relationships**.

3   Select the appropriate spouse. Then, in the editing panel, choose a relationship type from the **Relationship** pop-up menu.

Choosing a Status for a Couple's Relationship

The status of a couple's relationship will be "Ongoing" by default. If necessary, you can change this status. For example, if a couple gets divorced, you can change their relationship status to reflect this.

1 Go to the **Tree** tab on the People workspace and select the appropriate couple.

2 Click the **Person** tab; then click **Relationships**.

3 Select the appropriate spouse. Then, in the editing panel, choose a status from the **Status** pop-up menu.

Choosing a Relationship Between Parents and a Child

You can indicate a child's relationship to each of his or her parents (e.g., biological, adopted, foster).

1 Go to the **Tree** tab on the People workspace and select the appropriate individual.

2 Click the **Person** tab; then click **Relationships**.

3 Select the appropriate father or mother. Then, in the editing panel, choose a relationship from the **Relationship** pop-up menu.

Adding an Unrelated Individual

As you search for family members, you might find a person you suspect is related to you, but you have no proof. You can add this person to your tree without linking them to a specific family. Later on, if you find out that they are related, you can easily link them to the correct family.

1   Click the down arrow next to the **People** button on the main toolbar, and then choose **Add Person > Add Unrelated Person** from the pop-up menu.

2   Type the person's name (first, middle, and last). Then choose a gender from the pop-up menu and click **Add**.

Viewing a Timeline

Timelines can be a great tool for putting the life of your ancestor in context—historical and otherwise. Family Tree Maker has three timeline variations: events in an individual's life; events in the lives of his or her immediate family (such as birth, marriage, and death); and historical events.

1   Select the appropriate individual on the **Tree** tab of the People workspace, and then click the **Person** tab. Click **Timeline**. A chronological list of events is displayed—together with the person's age at the time of each event.

2   To display events for immediate family members, click the arrow next to the **Timeline** button and choose **Show Family Events**.
     Events for the individual are indicated by green markers, and events in his or her family are indicated by pink markers.

3   To display historical events, click the arrow next to the **Timeline** button and choose **Show Historical Events**.

Historical events are indicated by yellow markers.

4   To learn more about a historical event, select the event. A description appears in the right side of the workspace.

Creating Smart Stories™

Smart Stories is a tool that helps you quickly create stories about individuals and families using the facts, notes, and photos in your tree. And because Smart Stories are linked to the tree, you can edit a fact and the text in your story will be updated automatically. For example, if you find out that your grandfather's birth date is different than you thought, change it in your tree and the story will be updated at the same time.

Family Tree Maker can automatically generate a Smart Story for an individual. It will have an image of the person (if you've added a portrait), the individual's immediate family (children, spouses, parents, and siblings), and their life events. You can also create your own Smart Stories, starting with a blank page and adding your own images and text.

You can create Smart Stories on an individual's Media tab, the Media workspace, or the Publish workspace. All stories can be printed, exported, and included in family history books; however, if you upload your tree to Ancestry, Smart Stories created on the Publish workspace are considered reports and won't be uploaded.

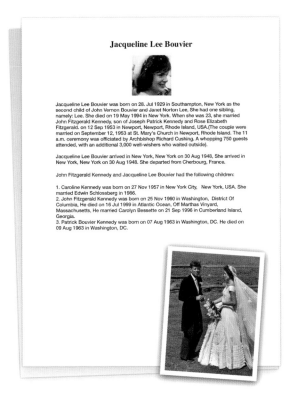

Creating a Smart Story as a Media Item

1   Select the individual you want to create a Smart Story for.

2   Do one of the following:

  • Go to the **Person** tab for an individual and click the **Media** tab at the bottom of the window. Click the arrow next to the

New button and choose **Create a New Smart Story** from the pop-up menu.

- Go to the Media workspace. Then Control-click a media item and choose **Create a New Smart Story** from the pop-up menu.

3 If you want Family Tree Maker to generate the story for you, click **Auto-populate Smart Story**. To create your own story, click **Start with blank page**.

4 Click **OK**.

Creating a Smart Story as a Report

1 Go to the **Collection** tab on the Publish workspace. In **Publication Types**, click **Other**.

2 Double-click the **Smart Story** icon. The editor opens.

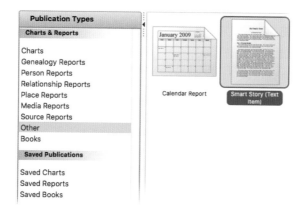

Tip: To access this Smart Story later, go to the Publish workspace and select **Saved Reports**.

Including a Short Biography

1 Place the cursor where you want to add a biography.

2 Click the **Facts** 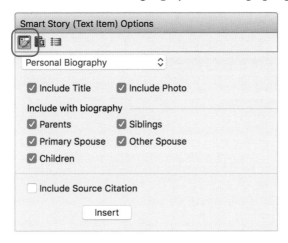 button on the Smart Stories toolbar. Then choose **Personal Biography** from the pop-up menu.

3 By default a title, photo, and the individual's immediate family (children, spouses, parents, and siblings) will be included. Deselect the checkboxes for items you don't want to include.

4 Click the **Insert** button.

Including Facts

1 Place the cursor on the page where you want to add a fact.

2 Click the **Facts** button on the Smart Stories toolbar. Then choose **Facts** from the pop-up menu.

3 Select the fact you want to add to your story. Below the fact, you'll see options of how the fact will be entered. You can create a sentence or add specific details.

4 Drag the text to your document or click the "plus" button.

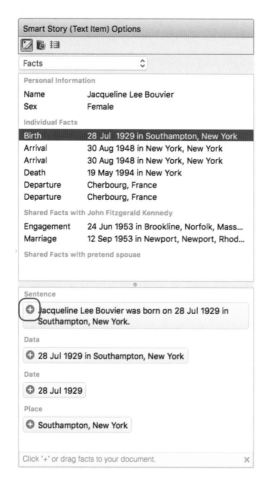

Tip: To include the facts, media items, or notes from another person in your tree, click the Index of Individuals icon next to the Pedigree Navigation bar at the top of the window and choose a different person.

Including Sources

1 Place the cursor on the page where you want to add a source.

2 Click the **Facts** button on the Smart Stories toolbar. Then choose **Fact Sources** from the pop-up menu.

3 Click the fact that has the source you want to add to your story. Below you'll see any associated source citations. If more than one source citation exists for a fact, you can choose it from a pop-up menu.

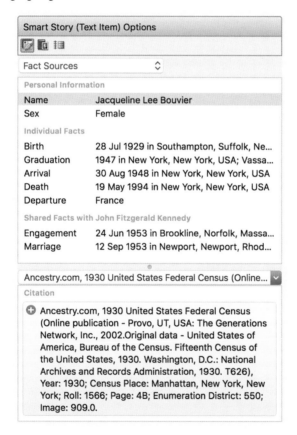

4 Drag the text to your document or click the "plus" button.

Including Notes

1 Place the cursor on the page where you want to add a note.

2 Click the **Facts** button on the Smart Stories toolbar. Then choose **Notes** from the pop-up menu.

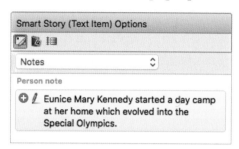

3 Drag the text to your document or click the "plus" button.

Including Images

1 Place the cursor on the page where you want the media item.

2 Click the **Media** button on the Smart Stories toolbar.

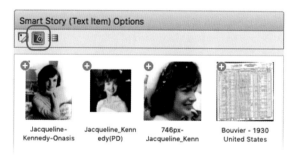

3 Drag the image to your document or click the "plus" button.

Creating Timelines

You can use facts in a person's life and historical events to create a timeline.

1 Place the cursor on the page where you want to add an event.

2 Click the **Timeline** button on the Smart Stories toolbar. Then choose an event type from the pop-up menu.

3 Click the event you want to add to your story. Below the event, you'll see options of how the event will be entered. You can create a sentence or add specific details.

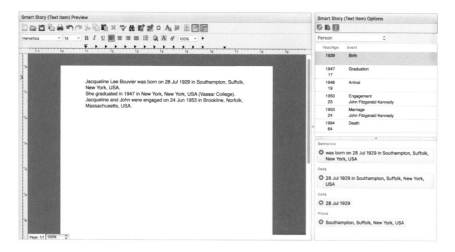

4 Drag the text to your document or click the "plus" button.

Editing Smart Stories Text

Smart Stories pull text directly from your tree. That means you don't have to worry about continually redoing your story; if information in your tree changes, your story will be updated automatically.

You can also edit text in Smart Stories. But, be aware that the text will no longer be linked to your tree and will not be updated automatically.

1   Move the cursor over the text you want to add, edit, or delete. You can tell which text is linked to your tree because it will be highlighted.

> Jacqueline Lee Bouvier was born on 28 Jul 1929 in Southampton, New York as the second child of John Vernon Bouvier and Janet Norton Lee. She had one sibling, namely: Lee. She died on 19 May 1994 in New York. When she was 23, she married John Fitzgerald Kennedy, son of Joseph Patrick Kennedy and Rose Elizabeth Fitzgerald, on 12 Sep 1953 in Newport, Newport, Rhode Island, USA (The couple were married on September 12, 1953 at St. Mary's Church in Newport, Rhode Island. The 11 a.m, ceremony was officiated by Archbishop Richard Cushing. A whopping 750 guests attended, with an additional 3,000 well-wishers who waited outside).

2   Double-click the text block. A message asks whether you want to convert the text to free form text (text that can be edited but is not linked to your tree).

3   Click **Yes** and edit the text.

Chapter Five

Documenting Your Research

Documenting sources—recording where you discovered a fact—is one of the most important aspects of your research. Sources are valuable for many reasons. When you cite a source, you are proving to others which records you based your facts on; if you eventually share your research with your family or other researchers, your family history may be judged for accuracy based on your sources. If your sources are detailed and correct, others will be able to follow in your investigative footsteps.

Each time you add information to your tree, you'll want to create a source and source citation that describe where you found it. For example, if you find your grandfather's birthplace on his World War I conscription papers, you'll create a source for the record when you add his birth date and birthplace.

Understanding Sources and Source Citations

If you're new to family history, you may not be familiar with sources and source citations. This section gives an explanation of each and also shows you some examples.

- A source is the unchanging facts about an item; for example, the author, title, and publication information for a book.

- Source citations are individual details that explain where you found a fact, such as the page number in a book.

To help you understand how sources and source citations work together, let's look at an example from the 1930 United States Federal Census. First, you would create a source for the census that includes information like this:

- A title—1930 United States Federal Census

- Where you located the source—www.ancestry.com

- Publishing details—Bureau of the Census. Washington, D.C.: National Archives and Records Administration, 1930.

As you can see, these details about the 1930 census won't change regardless of who or what you find in the records. However, because you'll find families and individuals in different locations throughout the census, each census fact will need its own source citation. A source citation for an individual in the 1930 census might include this information:

- Source—1930 United States Federal Census

- Source citation—Harold Reed household, Santa Clara Township, Santa Clara County, California. Roll: 219; Page: 14A; Enumeration district: 110.

A source citation for a different individual in the 1930 census might look like this. (Notice the source is the same as the previous example.)

- Source—1930 United States Federal Census

- Source citation—Michael Reed household, Kokomo Township, Beaver County, Oklahoma. Roll: 1892; Page: 5B; Enumeration district: 26.

Both individuals can be found in the 1930 census (the source), but the source citation for each individual has changed because the individuals were recorded in different places in the source.

Creating Sources

Family Tree Maker lets you create sources in two ways: using templates or a basic format. Source templates are useful because you don't have to guess which details need to be entered. Choose the type of source you're creating (for example an obituary) and Family Tree Maker displays the relevant fields. If you don't want to use a template (for example, because you have your own system of citation or you can't find a matching template), you can create a source by filling in the standard fields (author, title, and publisher) in the basic source format.

Adding a Source for a Fact

Usually, you will add a source as you create a source citation for a fact or event. This section focuses on adding a source while entering facts on the Tree tab in the People workspace.

Note: You need to create only one source for each item; you can use a source for as many source citations as necessary.

1   Go to the **Tree** tab on the People workspace.

2   In the editing panel, click the **New source citation** 🖼 button next to the fact you want to add a source to. Then choose **Add New Source Citation** from the pop-up menu.

3 The Add Source Citation dialog opens. To create a source using a template, follow the instructions in "Creating a Source from a Template" below. To create your own source, refer to the "Creating a Source Using the Basic Format" section on page 75.

Using Source Templates

Family Tree Maker includes more than 170 source templates to help you source everything from embroidered samplers and other artefacts to online databases and vital records. These source templates are based on the QuickCheck models in Elizabeth Shown Mills's book *Evidence Explained*—the leading reference work for citing genealogy sources.

Creating a Source from a Template

Using a source template is simple. To determine which template you should use, type keywords and choose from a list of suggestions, or view a list of all available templates and choose the one that fits best.

To choose a template using keywords

1 Open the Add Source Citation dialog and click **New**. The Add Source dialog opens. (See "Adding a Source for a Fact" on page 71.)

2 Type a keyword in the **Source Template** field and choose a template from the pop-up menu. To narrow the list, type multiple keywords. For example, "property" brings up eleven results, while "property deed" brings up one result.

3 The fields that appear now reflect the template you've selected. Fill in these fields as necessary and click **OK**.

You can now add a source citation for the fact (see page 77).

To choose a template from a list

1 Open the Add Source Citation dialog and click **New**. (If you need help, see "Adding a Source for a Fact" on page 71.) The Add Source dialog opens.

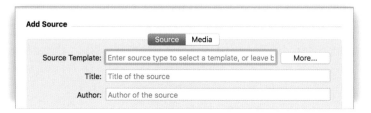

2 Click **More**.

3 In the **Source group** list, select the group that most closely matches the item you're sourcing. The categories list changes to reflect the selected source group.

4 Choose the appropriate category from the **Category** pop-up menu. The templates list changes to reflect the selected source group and category.

5 Choose a template from the **Template** pop-up menu. A description of the template is displayed beneath its title.

6 Click **OK** to return to the Add Source dialog; the fields that appear now reflect the template you've selected. Fill in these fields as necessary and click **OK**. You can now add a source citation for the fact (see page 77).

Creating a Source Using the Basic Format

If you don't want to use a source template, you can create a source by filling in some standard fields (such as author, title, and publisher) in the basic source format.

1 Open the Add Source Citation dialog and click **New**. (If you need help, see "Adding a Source for a Fact" on page 71.) The Add Source dialog opens.

2 Fill in the source fields as necessary:

- **Title.** Type the title of the source exactly as it appears in the source.

- **Author.** Type the author or originator's name.

- **Publisher Name.** Type the name of the publishing company.

- **Publisher Location.** Type the place of publication (for example, London, England).

- **Publish Date.** Type the copyright date for the source (usually only a year).

- **Source Repository.** Create a new repository or choose one from the pop-up menu.

  A repository is the location where an original source exists. This could be a library, an archive, a county record office, or a cousin's home. To create a repository, click **New**. Then type the name, address, email address, and phone number for the location.

- **Call Number.** Type a call number, if one exists.

  The call number is the number assigned to the source at the repository where you found the item. It could be a microfilm number, a Dewey Decimal system number, or a number from some other classification system unique to a particular library or archive.

- **Comments.** Type any comments about the source and the information found in it. This information will not be printed in your reports; it is for your personal reference. You might include a description of the item or even information about its legibility.

3 Click **OK**. You can now add a source citation for the fact (see page 77).

Creating Source Citations

After you create a source, you're ready to identify where in the source you found information by creating a source citation. Family Tree Maker lets you create source citations in a variety of ways; you'll need to decide which method is most effective for you.

Note: You can have more than one source citation for the same fact. For example, you might find an immigration date for your great-grandmother on a naturalisation record and a census record. You should make source citations for both records.

Adding a New Source Citation

Each time you add a fact to your tree, you should take a minute or two to document where you discovered the information, whether it's a book in a library or a record you found online. When you create a new source citation, you'll link it to a source and add any additional identifying information such as page or volume number.

1   Open the Add Source Citation dialog. (If you need help see "Adding a Source for a Fact" on page 71.)

2   Change the citation as necessary:

- **Source title.** From the pop-up menu, choose the source where you found the information.

- **Citation detail.** Type details about where you found the information in the source, such as a page number.

- **Citation text.** Type any additional information. For example, you might type a quote from a book or add a paraphrased summary of the source text.

- **Web address.** For online sources, enter the URL (the Internet address—you can copy it from the address field at the top of your Web browser window) where the information was found.

- **Include in reference note.** Select the **Citation text** checkbox to include the text from the Citation text field in printed reference notes. Select the **Web address** checkbox to include the source's URL in printed reference notes. (The source title and citation detail are always included in reference notes.)

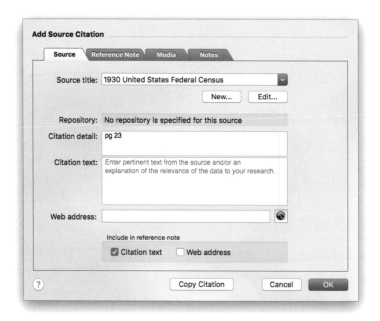

You can include a media item or note as part of a source citation. For instructions, see "Attaching a Media Item to a Source Citation" on page 81 and "Adding a Note to a Source Citation" on page 82.

3 Click **OK**.

Linking a Fact to an Existing Source Citation

If you've already created a citation for a source, such as a death certificate, you don't have to create another source citation for each fact or individual in the source. For example, if you find your grandparents' names and birthplaces in your aunt's death certificate, you don't have to create a new source citation for the death certificate; you can simply link these facts to the citation you already created.

1   Go to the **Tree** tab on the People workspace and select the appropriate individual. Then click the **Person** tab.

2   Select the fact you want to add a source citation to.

3   On the **Sources** tab of the editing panel, click the down arrow next to the **New** button and choose **Use Existing Source Citation** from the pop-up menu.

The **Find Source Citation** dialog opens.

4   Select the citation you want to link to from the list.

5   Click **Link to Citation**. The citation information now appears on the Sources tab.

Copying and Updating a Source Citation

If you need to create a source citation that is similar to one already in your tree, don't make a new citation. Simply copy the old one and update details as necessary (such as a page number). For example, if several family members are in the same city directory for Liverpool, you can create a source citation for one family, then copy and modify the source citation for other families in the directory.

1   Go to the **Tree** tab on the People workspace and select the appropriate individual. Then click the **Person** tab.

2   Select the fact you want to add a source citation to.

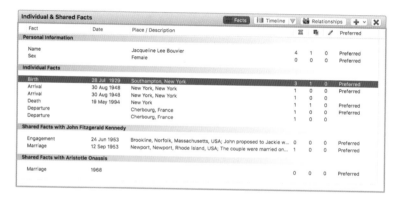

3   On the **Sources** tab of the editing panel, click the down arrow next to the **New** button and choose **Use Existing Source Citation** from the pop-up menu. The Find Source Citation dialog opens.

4   Select the citation you want to copy from the list.

5   Click **Create New Copy**. A citation link appears on the **Sources** tab. Now you can edit the citation without affecting the original.

6   Double-click the source citation to open it in an editing dialog. Make any necessary changes and click **OK**.

Replacing a Source Citation

If you need to replace a source citation with another one that is already in your tree, follow the same steps as for linking a fact to an existing citation (see page 78), but click the **Replace source citation** button on the **Sources** tab.

The **Find Source Citation** dialog will open, and you will be able to choose another citation.

Attaching a Media Item to a Source Citation

If you have an image or recording of a source, you can link it to a source citation. For example, you might have a scan of a marriage certificate or census record that you want to add to the source citation.

1   Double-click the source citation you want to add the media to.

2   Click the **Media** tab.

3 Do one of the following:

- If the media item is already in your tree, click **Link To Existing Media**. Select the item you want then click **OK**.

- To add a media item, click **Attach New Media**. Use the file management dialog to navigate to the media item. Then click **Open**.

4 Click **OK**.

Adding a Note to a Source Citation

You can use the Notes tab for additional information about a source that you weren't able to include elsewhere. For example, you can type a note about how you discovered a source or where the source is located.

1 Click the **Notes** tab in a source citation.

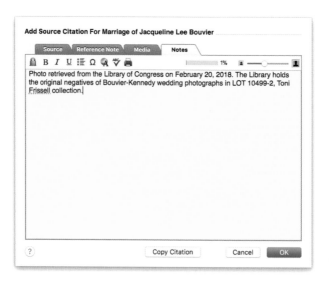

2 Type a note and click **OK**.

Using Source Repositories

With most sources, it's possible to specify the physical location where the original source can be found. This could be a library, a county record office, or an individual's home. This location is called the source's repository. Naturally, more than one source may reside in a repository. Therefore, you only need to enter information on each repository once. You can then link the appropriate sources to it rather than retyping the information for each source you create.

Adding a Repository

1   In the **Add/Edit Source** dialog (see "Adding a Source for a Fact" on page 71), click the **New** button next to the **Source Repositories** pop-up menu.

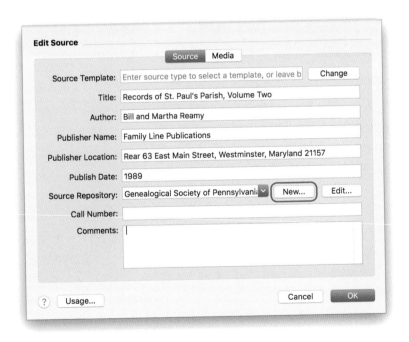

2   In the dialog that appears, enter the name, address, phone number, and email address of the location, and then click **OK**.

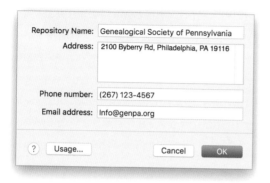

Managing Repositories

You can monitor the usage of repositories in your tree, as well as edit repository information, delete repositories, and add new ones. Changes you make to a repository are automatically applied to all the sources that are linked to it.

Reviewing Usage of a Repository

You may need to know how much information in your tree is sourced from a specific repository or to check that a repository has the correct sources linked to it. To do that, follow these steps:

1   Open the **Repositories** dialog (fig. 5-1 on the next page) by choosing **Manage Repositories** from the **Edit** menu.

2   Select a repository and click **Usage**. The **Repository Usage** dialog will appear with a list of sources linked to the selected repository and citations for these sources.

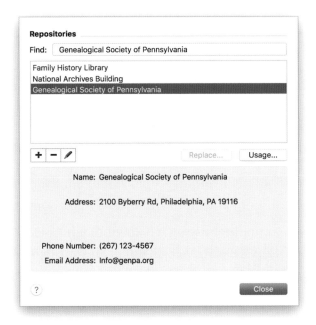

Figure 5-1. The Repositories dialog.

Replacing a Repository

You can change all of the occurrences of one repository to another repository. This merges the two repositories together as the second repository and deletes the first repository. All of the sources previously linked to the first repository will now be linked to the second repository. This allows you to combine duplicate repositories into a single repository without reassigning each source.

1   In the **Repositories** dialog, select the repository you want to replace.

2   Click the **Replace** button.

3 In the dialog that appears, select the repository to which you want to link all sources from the first repository.

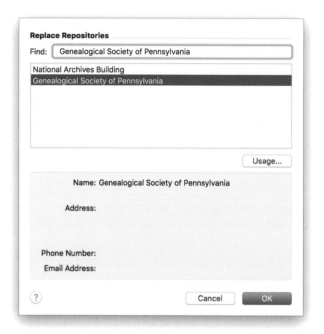

4 Click **OK**.

5 Click **Replace** in the confirmation dialog.

Editing Repository Information

To update or correct information about a particular repository, follow these steps:

1 Open the **Repositories** dialog by choosing **Manage Repositories** from the **Edit** menu .

2 Select the repository you want to edit.

3 Click the **Edit (pencil)** button.

4 Change the name, address, phone number, and/or email address, and then click **OK**.

Deleting a Repository

1   In the **Repositories** dialog, select the repository you want to delete.

2   Click the **Delete** (–) button.

3   In the message that appears, click **Delete and Unlink** to unlink all sources from the repository and delete it.

Chapter Six
Including Media Items

As you gather names, dates, and facts, you'll realise that these tell only part of your family's story. In order to really bring your ancestors to life, you'll want to illustrate your family history with photographs, important documents, and video and sound recordings.

What Media Items Can I Add to My Tree?

Photographs are usually the first thing that comes to mind when you want to illustrate your family history. But don't limit yourself; many personal objects can be scanned or photographed. Here are some items you might want to add to your tree:

- Important records, such as birth and marriage certificates, censuses, passports, diplomas, obituaries, and family Bibles.
- Photographs of heirlooms or items with sentimental value, such as jewellery, medals, artwork, christening outfits, and furniture.
- Images of ancestral homes and home towns, businesses, maps, cemeteries, and headstones.
- Family documents, such as letters, diaries, Christmas cards, condolence books, and newspaper and magazine articles.
- Audio recordings of oral histories and family stories.

Family Tree Maker helps you organise your multimedia items in one central location. You can link media items to specific individuals, record important notes about each item, use images in family tree charts, and more.

Adding Media Items

If you have a baby picture of your grandmother or a photo of your grandfather in his army uniform, you'll want to add it to your tree. You can add photos, audio files, and videos from your computer, scan documents directly into Family Tree Maker, or instantly import photos from your camera.

Adding a Media Item for an Individual

1   Go to the Tree tab on the People workspace and select the appropriate individual. Then click the Person tab.

2   Click the **Media** tab at the bottom of the workspace.

3   Click the down arrow next to the **New** button and choose **Add New Media** from the pop-up menu.

Note: When you add a media item to Family Tree Maker, the original file is not moved from its location on your computer.

4   Use the file management dialog to navigate to the media item you want to add to your tree. Then click **Open**.

Tip: You can select multiple media items by Command-clicking on each file.

A message asks whether you want to link the file to your tree or create a copy of the file.

5   Select **Copy this file** to create an additional copy of the file in the Family Tree Maker media folder, or select **Link to this file** to link to the file where it is on your computer.

Tip: Make copies of your media items if you want all your family heritage photos and other media items saved in one central location on your computer. This makes them easier to find and easier to back up.

6   Select the checkbox for the category you want this item to belong to; you can select multiple categories. (For more information see "Media Categories" on page 102.)

7   Click **OK**. The item is added to the individual's Media tab.

Scanning an Image into Your Tree

If you have images you'd like to add to your tree that aren't already on your computer, you can scan them directly into your tree.

When you scan an image, you need to choose the resolution in which the item will be saved. The higher the resolution, or DPI (dots per inch), the sharper your image will be—and the larger the size of the file that's created. If you plan to view your images online or send them by email, scan them at a lower resolution such as 72 to 150 DPI; if you want to print images in charts and reports, use a higher resolution such as 200 to 300 DPI.

1   Make sure your scanner is connected to your computer and turned on.

2 Click the **Media** button on the main toolbar. Then click the down arrow next to the button and choose **Scan Media** from the menu that appears. Family Tree Maker automatically searches for connected scanners.

3 Change any settings and click **Scan**.

4 In the dialog that appears, select the checkbox for the category you want this item to belong to; you can select multiple categories. (For more information, see "Media Categories" on page 102.)

5 Click **OK**. The item is added to the Media workspace.

Changing the Display of an Image

When you're viewing a photo, you can change how it's displayed by rotating it or zooming it in and out.

Go to the **Collection** tab on the Media workspace. Double-click a photo, or select the photo and then click the **Detail** tab.

Use these buttons in the image toolbar to change the display:

Click the **Rotate right** button to turn the image clockwise; click the **Rotate left** button to turn the image anticlockwise.

Click the **Size to fit** button to display the entire image in the current view.

Click the **Show actual size** button to show the actual size of the image. You can also choose a specific percentage from the **Fit Image** pop-up menu.

Entering Details for a Media Item

After you add a media item, it's a good idea to enter details about it such as a caption, date, and description.

1 Go to the **Collection** tab on the Media workspace. Double-click the media item, or select the image and click the **Detail** tab.

2 Change the image's details as necessary:

- **Caption.** Type a brief title for the item.

- **Date.** Type a date for the item. (Typically this is the date the item was created.)

- **Description.** Describe the media item in detail. For photos you can enter the names of individuals or information about the location depicted; for heirlooms you may want to explain what the item is and its significance to your family.

3 Select the **Private** checkbox to prevent this media item being exported or uploaded to your online Ancestry tree.

4   To assign a category to the item, click the **Edit** button next to
    the **Categories** field. Tick the checkbox for the category you
    want this item to belong to; you can select several categories if
    you wish. Click **OK** when you've finished.

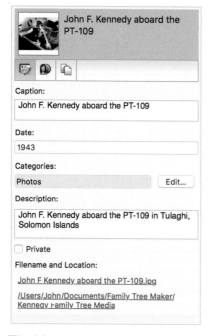

Tip: You can click the **Filename and Location** links to open the
file or the folder where the media item is.

Entering a Note About a Media Item

If you have information that won't fit in a media item's description,
you can enter it in the item's notes. For example, a photo of your
grandmother at her degree ceremony may include notes about her
university education and how you found the image.

1   Go to the **Collection** tab on the Media workspace. Double-click
    the media item you want to add a note to, or select the image
    and click the **Detail** tab.

2 Click the **Notes** tab at the bottom of the workspace and type the information.

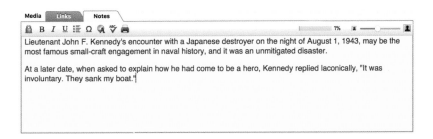

Note: For more information about using notes, see "Adding a Note for an Individual" on page 47.

Adding a Portrait for an Individual

If you want a photo of an individual to appear in charts and reports and on the People workspace, you'll need to add a portrait of that person.

1 Click the **People** button on the main toolbar. Make sure the individual you want to add a portrait to is the focus of the Tree tab or Person tab.

2 In the editing panel, Control-click the person silhouette and do one of the following:

- If the photo is already in your tree, choose **Link to Existing Picture**. The Find Media Item dialog opens. Select the photo you want then click **OK**.

- If you're adding a new photo, choose **Add New Picture**. Use the file management dialog to navigate to the photo you want. Then click **Open**.

Editing Photos with Photo Darkroom

Old photos may fade and deteriorate with time and wear. Fortunately, Family Tree Maker now comes with a photo repair tool integrated into your genealogy toolkit, allowing you to quickly and effortlessly edit your vintage photos without having to switch to an external image editor. Family Tree Maker's Photo Darkroom is all you need to revive and enhance old photos.

1   Go to the **Collection** tab on the **Media** workspace. Double-click the photo you want to repair, or select the photo and click the **Detail** tab.

2   Click the **Photo Darkroom** button. The photo opens in Photo Darkroom.

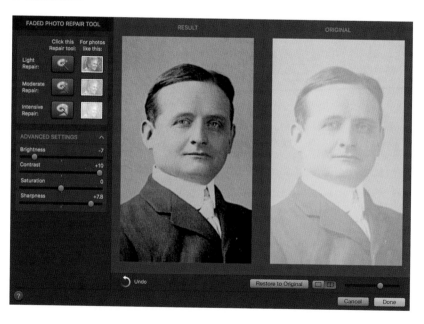

3   To view before and after images side by side as you are editing, click the two-pane button in the view control ▢ ▥. Both the Result and Original will be displayed.

4 Use the Faded Photo Repair Tool to make the image clearer. Depending on the degree of fading, click the **Light, Moderate,** or **Intensive** tool. You can click the tool several times to increase the effect.

5 If you want to make further changes to the photo, open the **Advanced Settings** section by clicking the disclosure triangle, and then drag the **Brightness, Contrast, Saturation** and **Sharpness** sliders while observing the changes in the Result view.

6 If you don't like the result of your changes, click the **Undo** button to discard them step by step. You can click the **Restore to Original** button to undo all the changes that you have made to the photo.

7 Click **Done** to apply your changes and return to the **Detail** tab of the **Media** workspace.

Note: The original photo is not modified. It is stored in the **Darkroom Originals** folder in your tree's media folder. If you want to use the original photo in your tree, without the changes that you have made to it, just open the photo in Photo Darkroom at any time, and then click the **Restore to Original** button.

Linking a Media Item to Multiple Individuals

You may have a family photo that includes several individuals in your tree. You don't have to add the picture to each individual; simply add it once to the Media workspace, then link it to the necessary individuals. You can also link media items to specific facts. For example, if you have a photograph of the ship on which your grandparents emigrated to Australia, you can link the picture to your grandparents and their emigration fact.

1   Go to the **Collection** tab on the Media workspace. Then double-click the item you want to link to multiple individuals, or select the item and click the **Detail** tab.

2   Click the **Links** tab at the bottom of the workspace. Then click the **New** button and choose **Link to Person**.

The Link Selected Media dialog opens.

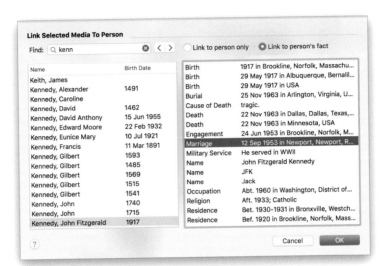

3 In the **Name** column, select the individual you want to link the media item to.

4 Do one of the following:

- To link the item to a person, select **Link to person only**. (You can link to only one person at a time.)

- To link the item to a specific fact (such as birth), select **Link to person's fact**. Then select the fact in the list.

5 Click **OK**.

Tip: If you mistakenly link a media item to an individual, you can unlink it on the Links tab. Select the appropriate individual and then click the **broken link** button on the Links toolbar.

Managing Media Items

Occasionally you might need to do some maintenance work with your media items such as changing file names or assigning categories.

Opening a Media Item from Family Tree Maker

If you need to edit an image or open a document in your tree, you can open it in its default application without leaving Family Tree Maker.

Go to the **Collection** tab on the Media workspace. Double-click a media item or select the item and click the **Detail** tab.

 Click the **Open file** button in the image toolbar. The media item opens in the file's default application. If you edit the media item and save your changes, the modified file will be linked to Family Tree Maker.

Changing a Media Item's File Name

Family Tree Maker lets you change a media item's file name on your computer. This can be useful if you've imported a tree and its media files have generic names; you can use Family Tree Maker to change their file names to something more identifiable.

1   Go to the **Collection** tab on the Media workspace. Control-click a media item and choose **Rename Media File** from the shortcut menu.

2   Type the new name for the file and click **Rename**.

Arranging an Individual's Media Items

When you add media items for an individual, they are arranged in alphabetical order (according to their caption). You can change the order in which they appear on the individual's Media tab. For example, you may want to display the pictures in chronological order.

1 Go to the **Person** tab on the People workspace and select the appropriate individual.

2 Click the **Media** tab at the bottom of the workspace. The tab shows thumbnails of any media items you've linked to this individual.

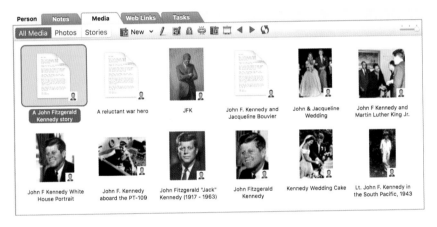

Use these buttons in the media toolbar to change the display order:

 Select the item you want to move. Then click the **Move Media Forward** and **Move Media Backward** arrows to rearrange the media items. The items will remain in the order you set.

 Click the **Auto Sort Media** button to arrange media items back in alphabetical order of their captions.

Click the **Photos** and **Stories** buttons to view only images or only text items respectively. Click the **All Media** button to display all of the media items linked to the individual.

Media Categories

As you add each media item to your tree, you can assign it to categories. These categories make your media items easier to search for, sort, and view.

Creating a Category

You can use the default categories, modify them, or create your own. If you decide to create your own categories, you might want to set up a system before you add your media items. For example, you may want to have event categories (e.g., Weddings, Birthdays, Travel) or categories based on item types (e.g., Photos—Portraits, Videos—Holidays).

1   Go to the **Collection** tab on the Media workspace. In the media editing panel, click the **Edit** button next to the **Categories** field. The Categories dialog opens.

2   Click the **Add** (+) button.

3   Type a name for the category and click **OK**.

Assigning a Category to Multiple Items

Family Tree Maker lets you assign categories to a group of items at the same time.

1   Go to the **Collection** tab on the Media workspace.

2   Select the media items you want to assign a category to. You can select multiple media items by Command-clicking on each one you want.

3   Click the down arrow next to the **Media** button on the main toolbar and choose **Categorize Media** from the pop-up menu.

4 In the Categorize Media window, you can choose categories for each media item one by one or for all selected media items at once.

Creating a Slide Show

You can create a slide show of pictures you've included in your tree—and even add a soundtrack. You can view your completed slide shows using *QuickTime*.

1 Click the **Media** button on the main toolbar. Then click the down arrow next to the button and choose **Create Slide Show** from the menu that appears.

Tip: You can create a slide show for a specific individual by clicking the **Create slide show** button on the individual's Media tab.

2 Change the slide show options as necessary:

- **Title.** Type a name for the slide show. (This will also be the item's file name on your computer.)

- **Images to Include.** To include pictures from a specific category, choose the category from the pop-up menu. If you opened this dialog by clicking the **Create slide show** button on an individual's Media tab, select the **Include relationship media** checkbox to include images linked to the person's relationships and select the **Include fact media** checkbox to include images linked to facts associated with the person.

• **Image Caption.** Choose what text is displayed for images. Choose **None** to hide captions displayed; choose **Use Captions Only** to display image captions; choose **Use Filenames Only** to display file names; choose **Use Captions or Filenames** to display captions (if no caption has been entered, the file name will be displayed).

Click the **Font** button to select a font style, size, and colour for captions and file names used in the slide show.

• **Movie Size.** Choose the display size from the pop-up menu.

Note: The larger the movie, the more memory required.

- **Movie Quality.** Choose the display quality from the pop-up menu.

  Note: The higher the movie quality, the more memory required.

- **Transition Delay.** Choose the number of seconds each image will be displayed for.

- **Sound Track.** To add music to the slide show, click **Sound Track** and choose **Browse** from the pop-up menu. Then locate the audio file (MP3) you'd like to use and click **Open**.

3 Click **Continue**. Now you can change the order in which images appear or delete images you don't want.

4 Click **Continue**. A preview of the slide show opens.

5 Do one of the following:

- To view the finished slide show in *QuickTime*, select **Launch slide show with Finder**.

- To save the slide show to your tree, select **Add slide show to the media collection**.

6 Click **Finish**.

7 If you have selected the **Add slide show to the media collection** checkbox, the **Save to Media Folder** dialog appears. Click the checkbox for the category you want this slide show to belong to; you can select multiple categories. Click **OK** to add the slide show to the Media workspace.

8 If you have not selected the **Add slide show to the media collection** checkbox, the **Save movie** dialog appears. Choose a location and click **Save**.

Printing a Media Item

1 Go to the **Collection** tab on the Media workspace and select the item you want to print.

2 Click the **Print** button on the main toolbar and choose **Print Media Item** from the shortcut menu.

3 When prompted choose a printer, select the number of copies, and choose a page range.

4 Click **Print**.

Chapter Seven
Using Maps

As you gather the names and dates of important events in your ancestors' lives, you'll also record the locations where these events took place—the villages, towns, cities, and countries that shaped their daily lives.

Often, these places exist only as names in a report or on a pedigree chart. Family Tree Maker brings these ancestral homelands to life by letting you virtually visit each place in your tree. For example, you can see satellite images and maps of the town in Denmark where your grandfather was born, the house in Birmingham where your great-grandparents lived, or even the beach where you went swimming with your cousins every summer.

Every time you enter a location for a fact or event, Family Tree Maker adds it to a "master list" of locations. To view this master list, just go to the Places workspace. You can then view maps and satellite images of a location, identify individuals in your tree who are associated with certain locations, and more.

Viewing a Map

The interactive online maps in Family Tree Maker are easy to navigate using a few simple tools. You can zoom in and out on the map and change the type of map you're viewing.

Note: You must be connected to the Internet to view these maps.

1   Click the **Places** button on the main toolbar. To open a map, select a location in the **Places** panel.

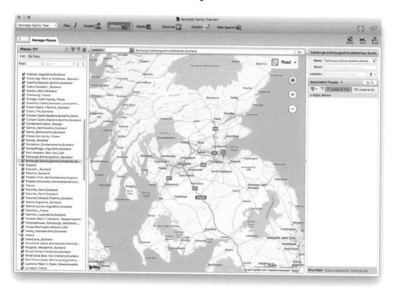

There are four map types. The **Road** map type appears by default with the location centred and indicated by a red marker. **Aerial** looks straight down at the location. **Bird's eye** provides a 3D angled view. And **Streetside** is the view you'd have if you were standing on the spot. To change the map type, click the map view drop-down menu in the upper-right corner and choose the view you want.

2   Choose **Aerial** to see a satellite image of the location.

Microsoft Bing Maps

Family Tree Maker has teamed up with Microsoft® *Bing*™ *Maps* to let you access some of the most exciting technology available today. *Bing Maps* takes you beyond typical road maps by combining them with special satellite and aerial imagery to let you experience the world as it looks today.

As you visit different locations, you'll notice that the level of detail for each town, region, or country varies. In some areas you can zoom in close enough to see cars, rooftops, and street junctions; in other areas your view will disappear when you get within a mile of the location. Fortunately, *Bing Maps* is updated regularly and regions that may not have many images now will do in the future. The most detailed views are of the United States, the United Kingdom, Canada, and Australia.

3 To get a 3D view of a location, click **Bird's eye**. Click the arrows on either side of the compass tool to change the direction of the view.

Note: Bird's-eye view is available only for certain parts of the world.

4 To turn the display of map labels such as street names on and off in Aerial and Bird's eye views, click the map view drop-down menu, choose **Aerial**, and click the **Labels** switch control at the bottom of the list.

5 Choose **Streetside** to explore places as if you were there. This view is not available for all areas of the world. See "Using Streetside View" on page 112 for more information.

Moving Around a Map

You can quickly change the part of the map you're viewing by dragging it. Move the pointer over the map. When the pointer changes to a hand, click and drag the map in any direction you want.

Zooming In and Out on a Map

You can use the zoom icons in the map tools to zoom in and out on a map.

1 Click the plus ⊕ icon to zoom in one level at a time.

2 Click the minus ⊖ icon to zoom out one level at a time.

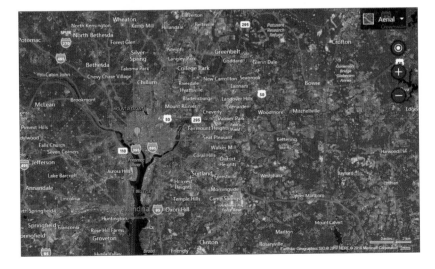

Using Streetside View

1 Look for Streetside locations by clicking the map view drop-down menu and choosing **Streetside**. The pointer changes to the blue man  icon wherever Streetside views are available.

2 Streetside view is not available for all locations. On the map, locations that can be viewed from the Streetside perspective are shaded blue. If there are any such locations in the display area, the Streetside pointer icon is blue. Click the location for which you want to get the Streetside view.

3 If there are no locations with Streetside view in the visible part of the map, the Streetside pointer icon turns red. Scroll the map until the pointer turns blue or click the Streetside item in the map view menu again to switch off the Streetside pointer icon and blue street markings.

4 In Streetside view, use these means of navigation:

- Click the plus and minus buttons to zoom in and out.

- Click the arrows in the view to move along the streets.

- Drag the view to rotate the line of sight and look up or down.
- Click the compass ⏵ icon to reset the view to looking due north.
- Click the **Show location on a map** ⬆ button to show the current Streetside location on a Road map. The location is marked by an orange diamond, and the field of vision is also shown. To jump to another location, drag the map so that the location you want comes under the orange diamond. To hide the Road map, click the **Hide map** button ⬇ .

5 To leave Streetside view and return to the view you were in before entering Streetside (Road or Aerial), click the Close button in the top-right corner.

Finding Places of Interest

Family Tree Maker helps you search for places of interest such as libraries and cemeteries near important places in your family history. If you're planning a research trip, you can use the maps to view all the cemeteries and churches in your ancestor's home town before you set off. You can also type in other attractions and sights—try searching "hotel" or "park", for example.

1 Click the **Places** button on the main toolbar.

2 If you've already entered the location in your tree, select it in the **Places** panel; otherwise, type the location's name in the blank field above the map on the right.

3 Choose a location type (such as libraries) from the pop-up menu and click **Go**. (You can also type in your own search term in the Location field.) Blue drawing pins appear for all the items that match your search.

4   Move the pointer over a drawing pin to see a name and address
    for the location (if available).

Printing a Map

You can print maps directly from the software, whether it's an aerial
shot of your ancestor's farm or the migration path your great-uncle
took across North America.

1   On the Places workspace, open the map you want to print. The
    display window shows what part of the map will be printed. You
    may need to resize the workspace to display more of the map.

2   In the main toolbar click the **Print** button and choose **Print
    Map** from the pop-up menu. The Print dialog opens.

3   When prompted, choose a printer, select the number of copies,
    and choose a page range.

4   Click **Print**.

Viewing Locations in Groups

On the Places workspace, you can view locations in an alphabetical list or grouped together by country, county, city, and so on. If you have hundreds of places in your tree, groups make it easier to quickly find the one you're interested in. An additional benefit is that you can see all people who are associated with a specific country or city with one click.

Note: To make sure locations are grouped together correctly, you'll need to resolve any place name errors. For help, see "Standard Locations" on page 265.

1   In the Places workspace, click the **Alphabetical/Groups** button to switch between showing places in an alphabetical list or by groups.

2   To see all places within a group, click its disclosure triangle. To expand all groups, click the **Expand All Nodes** button.

Viewing People and Facts Linked to a Location

Family Tree Maker lets you view all the events that took place at a certain location and the people associated with each event.

1 Click the **Places** button on the main toolbar.

2 Select a location in the **Places** panel. On the right side of the workspace, you'll see the selected location and the individuals who have life events associated with it.

Tip: If you're viewing locations in groups, you can see all the people and events for a group by clicking the **Linked to All** button and then clicking a country, state, county, or city in the list of places. Or view people and events just for a particular selected location by clicking the **Linked to This** button.

3 Do one of the following:

- To see the event that occurred at this location for a specific individual, click the disclosure triangle next to the individual.

- To see the events that occurred at this location for all the individuals, click the **Expand** button on the toolbar and choose **Expand All**. (Click the **Collapse all** button to close all the events.)

- To always have all people and events related to the selected location showing, click the **Expand** button on the toolbar and select **Expand All on Load**.

Creating Migration Maps

Maps can be extremely useful when tracing an ancestor. You can see at a glance all the locations that are connected with a specific individual or family, track migration patterns, and maybe discover where to locate more records.

Creating a Migration Map for an Individual

1 Click the **Places** button on the main toolbar. In the Places panel, choose "By Person" from the **List** pop-up menu.

2 Select the individual whose migration map you want to see. A map appears in the display area; the individual's birthplace is indicated by a green marker and death place by a dark red marker.

   To the right of the map is every fact you've entered for the individual—and its location.

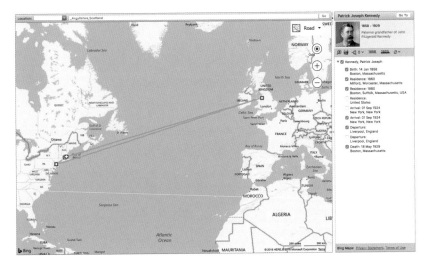

3 Select the checkbox next to a fact to include its location in the migration map.

4 Position the pointer over a marker to see the location's name and the fact associated with it.

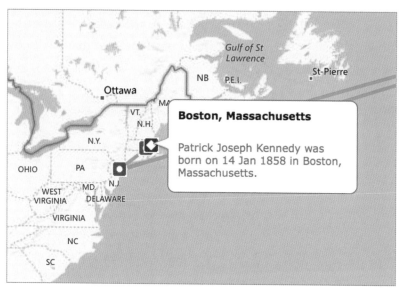

Creating a Migration Map for a Family

1 Click the **Places** button on the main toolbar. In the Places panel, choose "By Person" from the **List** pop-up menu and select an individual.

2 To view the locations associated with the individual's immediate family (parents, siblings, spouse, and children), click the **Include immediate family** button in the mapping toolbar.

3 Select an individual on the right side of the map to highlight his or her life events on the map. The migration path for the individual is indicated by a thick line.

Tip: You can change the colour of a migration path by clicking the line colour buttons in the mapping toolbar.

4 To view locations associated with an individual's ancestors (up to four generations), click the **Ancestor generations** button in the mapping toolbar and choose the number of generations from the pop-up menu.

A map appears in the display area: birthplaces are indicated by green markers and death places by dark red markers; the migration path for each individual is indicated by a coloured line.

Entering GPS Coordinates

Although the online maps are able to recognise most places, there are times when it won't be able to identify a location. Perhaps your grandmother is buried in a small rural graveyard or census records show your ancestors living in a village that no longer exists. You can set a location's exact position using GPS (Global Positioning System) coordinates.

1 Click the **Places** button on the main toolbar. In the Places panel, select the location you want to add GPS coordinates to.

2 Place the insertion point in the **Location** field and click the **Location calculator** button that appears.

3 Type the coordinates for the location in degrees:minutes:seconds, degrees:decimal minutes, or decimal degrees. Then click OK.

Entering a Display Name for a Location

Recording locations in a complete and consistent manner is an important part of creating a quality family history. Unfortunately, long location names can clutter your reports and charts. To avoid this problem, you can enter your own shortened or abbreviated display names. For example, instead of using Bronxville, Westchester, New York, USA, for a birthplace, you can enter Bronxville, NY, as the display name.

1 In the Places panel, select the location you want to change.

2 Type a display name in the **Short** field.

Chapter Eight
Researching Your Tree Online

As you enter stories and facts, you'll probably notice that more information about your family is waiting to be discovered—perhaps it's the burial location of your grandfather or the wedding certificate for your aunt and uncle. Family Tree Maker can help you fill in these gaps in your research with hints—behind-the-scenes searches of Ancestry and FamilySearch.

You can also search for information on RootsWeb.com, or any of your favourite websites. If you find info that matches a family member, you can quickly add it to your tree—without leaving Family Tree Maker.

Ancestry Hints

Once your FTM tree is uploaded to Ancestry to create a linked Ancestry tree, Family Tree Maker automatically searches thousands of databases on Ancestry looking for information that matches people in your tree. When a possible match is found, a green leaf or "hint" appears next to an individual in the tree viewer and editing panel on the People workspace. You can view the results when it's convenient, and if the information is relevant, you can add it to your tree.

FamilySearch Hints

FamilySearch, the largest genealogy organisation in the world, is operated by The Church of Jesus Christ of Latter-day Saints. Millions of people use FamilySearch records, resources, and services each year to learn more about their family history.

Family Tree Maker 2017 provides you with direct access to FamilySearch's Family Tree database of more than one billion names. You can get automatic match suggestions (hints), search the database, and merge any useful records you find into your own tree, just like you can with records you find on Ancestry's databases.

> Note: If you don't want Family Tree Maker to automatically search Ancestry or FamilySearch when you're connected to the Internet, you can turn this feature off. To do this, choose **Family Tree Maker 2017>Preferences**, click **General** and uncheck options for hints.

Viewing Ancestry and FamilySearch Hints

If Family Tree Maker finds records or trees on Ancestry or FamilySearch that might match an individual in your tree, you'll see a "hint" icon—a green leaf or a blue square respectively—next to the person on the People workspace. Hold the pointer over the icon to see the number of records and trees that were found.

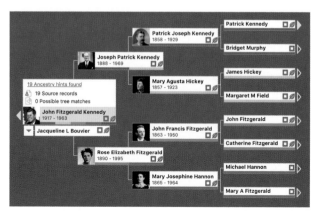

Note: To view Ancestry Hints you must have an Internet connection, be logged in to your Ancestry account, and have your FTM tree linked to your Ancestry tree. To get hints for new people you add to your tree, keep your FTM and Ancestry trees synced. To view the actual records and images, you must have an Ancestry subscription.

1 Go to the **Tree** tab on the People workspace. In the tree viewer or editing panel, click a hint icon.

2 Select a hint that interests you from the hint results list. If the record matches someone in your family, you can add it to your tree. (See "Adding Records to a Tree" on page 130.) If the record does not match anyone in your tree, you can ignore it. (See "Ignoring Hints" below.)

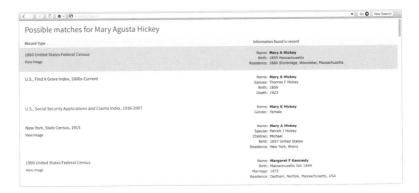

Ignoring Hints

If a hint is not relevant to someone in your tree, you can ignore it so it won't appear in your list of hints and matches again.

1 Access the hints for an individual.

2 On the Possible Matches page, click the item you want to ignore.

3 On the Search Results Detail toolbar, click the **Ignore record** icon (a circle with a diagonal line through it).

The **Ignore record** icon turns to a selected state when you click it to indicate the hint is being ignored.

Viewing Ignored Hints

If you've chosen to ignore specific hints for an individual, you can still view them at a later time.

1 Using the mini pedigree tree or Index of Individuals button, select the individual whose ignored hints you'd like to view.

2 Click the **Web Search** button on the main toolbar.

3 Select **Ancestry** or **FamilySearch** in the Search Locations list.

4 Click the down arrow next to the **Web Search** button and choose **View Ignored Records** from the pop-up menu.

5 To take the hint off the Ignore list, click the **Ignore record** icon (a circle with a diagonal line through it) to deselect it.

Searching Ancestry

You don't have to wait for Ancestry Hints to help you discover facts about your family, you can search the website any time you like.

Note: Although anyone can view Ancestry search results, you must have a subscription to view the actual records and images.

1 Click the **Web Search** button on the main toolbar.

2 Select Ancestry in the Search Locations list. Use the mini pedigree tree or Index of Individuals button to select the individual you want to research.

What Can I Find on Ancestry.com?

Ancestry.com is the world's largest online family history resource with more than 20 billion historical records—and more being added all the time. Here's a sample of the wealth of information available on Ancestry:

- A complete U.S. census collection (1790–1940). You'll also find census records for the UK, Australia, Canada, and other countries.
- Immigration records and passenger lists from 1820 to 1960.
- Birth, marriage, and death records going back as far as the 16th century.
- More than 550 million military records from the 1600s to the Vietnam War and beyond.
- More than 150 million pages from historical newspapers as far back as the 1700s.
- More than 20,000 local histories, memoirs, diaries, and biographies.
- Thousands of photos from the Library of Congress, maps beginning in the 1500s, and photographs dating back to the mid-1800s.
- Over 90 million family trees from all over the world—created by researchers just like you. Within these trees you'll find 330 million photographs, scanned documents, and stories.

Notice that some fields have been completed for you already.

By some fields you'll see an Exact checkbox. Use these to limit your searches to records that match your search terms exactly. Start by typing only one or two search terms, such as name and location.

3 Add or delete names, dates, and places as necessary.

4 To display records for a specific country or ethnicity first in your search results, choose a command from the **Collection Focus** pop-up menu.

5 To limit your search results to a specific type of record:

- Select the **Historical records** checkbox to search for birth records, censuses, military and immigration records, etc.

- Select the **Stories & publications** checkbox to search for member-submitted stories, newspapers, and other publications.

- Select the **Family trees** checkbox to search trees submitted by Ancestry members.

- Select the **Photos & maps** checkbox to search maps, historical images, and member-submitted photos.

6 Click **Search**.

7 If you get a large number of search results or matches, click the
Edit Search button to narrow your search. Try adding more
dates, a gender, or a spouse's name. (You can also narrow your
search by clicking a category link on the left.) If you get too few
results or no matches, delete one or more of your search terms
to widen your search.

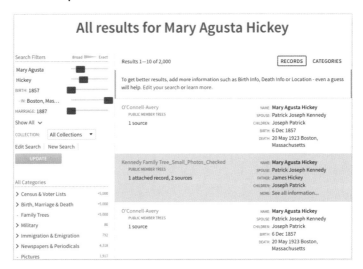

8 Select a search result to see the record or index. The tab at the
bottom of the workspace lets you compare, side by side, the facts
in your tree with the details found in the highlighted record.

9 If the information matches what you already know about the
individual and his or her family, you can add the information to
your tree. (See "Adding Records to a Tree" on page 130.)

Ancestry Search Tips

Ancestry automatically includes name variations, abbreviations, and nicknames when it searches for records. But if you're searching for an elusive ancestor, try these tips to get the most out of your searches:

- **Use wildcards.** Wildcards represent unknown letters in a name. Use an asterisk for up to six characters; a search for "fran*" will return results for Fran, Franny, Frank, Frannie, and Frankie. Use a question mark for a single character; a search for "Hans?n" will return matches such as Hansen and Hanson.

- **Search for similar-sounding names.** You can search for last names that "sound like" the one you're looking for. For example, a search for Smith would return Smithe, Smyth, and Smythe. To do so, click the "Exact" link under the individual's surname. Then select the **Sounds like, Soundex,** and **Similar** checkboxes.

- **Estimate dates.** Not sure of the exact date of an event? Make an educated guess; you'll get better results than if you leave the field blank.

- **Narrow your search by content.** Search for a specific type of content, such as a family trees, historical records, or maps. To do this, select the necessary checkboxes at the bottom of the search page.

- **Search in specific collections.** Ancestry has special collections focused on countries and ethnicities. If you're looking for an individual who lived in only one country, you can narrow your search to that location. Simply choose an option from the "Collection Focus" pop-up menu.

FamilySearch Search Tips

- **Search for name variations.** Try searching for variations in spelling or different variations of the same name. You can also try nicknames, different middle names and abbreviations.

- **Use wildcards.** Wildcards allow you to replace letters in a person's name and check for multiple spellings in a single search. A question mark (?) replaces a single character, and an asterisk (*) replaces multiple characters. For example, searching for Sm?th will return results for Smith, Smeth, or even Smythe. A search for Joh* will find matches such as John, Johnson, or Johnathon.

- **Estimate dates.** Not sure of the exact date of an event? Make an educated guess; you might get better results than if you leave the field blank.

- **Provide less information.** Adding too much information to your search may exclude results that don't have all that information, or where some of the information differs. For example, try entering just a name and one event, or use only the name if it's not very common.

- **Provide more or different information.** Adding more information may help to find a record that matches more closely.

- **Use exact searching carefully.** Bear in mind that using the "Match All Exactly" checkbox returns fewer results. On the other hand, exact searching might be very helpful, limiting the results to people who lived in a specific place and time.

- **Use other alphabets.** If the person was from a country with a different alphabet, try looking for the name written in the person's native language.

Important: You can use the Find feature to find only deceased people in the FamilySearch Family Tree; you cannot look up living people.

Searching FamilySearch

You can search the FamilySearch Family Tree database without waiting for FamilySearch hints to appear. This will produce a list of possible matches to people in your tree. You can then review the possible matches and merge any information that you find to be relevant into your Family Tree Maker tree.

1   Go to the **Web Search** workspace.

2   In the Search Locations list, select FamilySearch.

3   In the search form, enter information about an individual for whom you want to search.

4   Click **Find**. The search results appear.

5   Select a search result and look through the person's data in the Search Results Detail area. If this is the individual you were looking for, you can add the information you have found to your tree. (See "Adding Records to a Tree" below.)

Adding Records to a Tree

When you find a relevant record or family tree on Ancestry or FamilySearch, you can add the information directly to your tree using the Web Merge Wizard. You can choose the pieces of information you want to add and whether that information will be "preferred" or "alternate". The wizard can even include record images and sources for you automatically.

> Note: It is always a good idea to save a backup of your tree file before making major changes using Web Merge.

1   In the Web Search workspace, access the record that you want to add to your tree.

2 Make sure the individual you want to add the record to is selected in the Person from Your Tree section. If you need to add the record to a different person, click the **Select a different person** button (an index card) in the toolbar. Select an individual and click **OK**.

The bottom of the workspace displays the information in your tree compared side by side with the information found in the online record or tree.

3 Click **Merge**. The Web Merge Wizard will launch. Depending on the type of record you've accessed, the wizard may contain multiple dialogs.

The left side of the dialog lists the names of the people included in the record you are adding. As you move through the wizard, each individual will be highlighted as you make decisions about his or her information. Next to the individuals' names, you'll see two columns: the Person from My Tree column shows the information you already have in your tree; the Person from Web Search column shows the information from the record.

4 Use the buttons next to the facts in the two columns to determine how each fact will be added:

- To keep a fact and mark it as "preferred", select the button next to the fact. The corresponding fact for the other individual will be added as an alternate fact unless you choose to discard it.

- To remove a fact, click the arrow next to the **Alternate** heading and choose **Discard** from the pop-up menu. This fact will not be added to your tree. Though you may choose to discard some facts for a person, it is usually a good idea to keep all facts in case they turn out to be relevant.

If you discard a fact, you still have the option to add its source, media, and notes to your tree by clicking the corresponding checkboxes in the **Keep** group.

5   Click **Continue** and do the following:

- If the individual you want to add has parents, spouses, or children associated with the record, the wizard asks if you want to add the information found for the first additional family member. Go on to step 6.

- If the individual doesn't have siblings or parents associated with the record, click the **Continue** button to go to the Summary dialog. Skip ahead to step 8.

6 Choose what you want to do with each family member. You can ignore the person, add the person as a new individual in your tree, or merge the person with an existing individual in your tree.

The details about the additional family members appear in the Person from Web Search column, while the information you already have in your tree appears in the Person from My Tree column. You can compare the information you have with what Family Tree Maker has found. If more than one individual appears in the Person from My Tree column, you will need to select the individual with whom you want to merge the new information.

7 Click **Continue** and complete step 6 for every name in the record until all additional family members have been looked through. When you have made decisions for each family member, the Summary dialog opens.

8 Verify your selections in the Summary dialog. Click **Merge**. A message tells you when the information has been added successfully to your tree. Click **OK** to close the message.

Note: You *cannot* undo a merge. However, if you made a mistake, you can simply delete the facts or sources that you added.

Searching Online with Family Tree Maker

With Family Tree Maker, you have a convenient starting point for researching and expanding your family history—without interrupting your work. You can explore the Web using any of your favourite search engines or genealogy websites. Then use the "Web clipping" tool to select text and images you're interested in and add them to individuals in your tree.

1 Click the **Web Search** button on the main toolbar. Using the mini pedigree tree or Index of Individuals button, choose the individual whose information you want to search for.

2 In **Search Locations**, select the website you want to search, or type a website in the address field of the Web browser. The website opens.

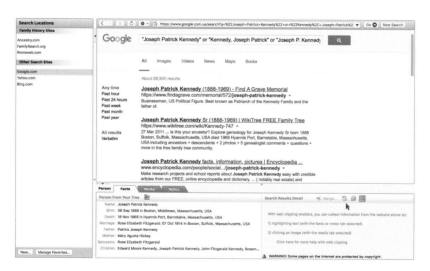

3 Look for information on your ancestors just as you would if you were performing any kind of online search.

Copying Online Facts

If you find details on a website that you'd like in your tree, you can use the "Web clipping" tool. In some cases, Family Tree Maker will recognise the type of information you're viewing and will give you relevant fields to choose from. For example, if you add information from the United States Social Security Death Index, you'll have the option to add the text to a name, Social Security Number, birth fact, or death fact.

1   Click the **New Search** button.

2   Go to the website you want to copy facts from.

3   If you want to link the facts to a different person, click the **Select a different person** button in the **Person from Your Tree** section which is located at the bottom of the window. Select an individual and click **OK**.

4   Click the **Facts** tab at the bottom of the workspace. On the Search Results Detail toolbar, click the **Enable web clipping** button.

5   Move the pointer over text on the website until the pointer turns into an I-beam. Highlight the text you want to copy. A pop-up menu appears.

6 Choose a fact from the **Insert Fact** pop-up menu. For example, you can choose the birthplace fact. The highlighted information now appears in the Search Results Detail section.

Tip: You can copy multiple facts before adding the information to your tree; you don't need to add each fact individually.

7 When you have selected all the information you want, click **Merge**. The Web Merge Wizard will launch.

8 Choose how you want the information to be merged into your tree:

- To keep a fact and mark it as "preferred", select the button next to the fact. The corresponding fact for the other individual will be added as an alternate fact unless you choose to discard it.

- To remove a fact, click the arrow next to the **Alternate** heading and choose **Discard** from the pop-up menu. This fact will not be added to your tree. Though you may choose to discard some facts for a person, it is usually a good idea to keep all facts in case they turn out to be relevant.

9 Click **Summary** to see how the information will be added to your tree. If necessary, click **Edit** to enter a source citation for the information. (The default source citation is the URL, or Web address, where the information was located.)

10 Click **Merge**. A message tells you when the information has been added successfully. Click **OK** to close the message.

Copying an Online Image

You may find family photos or historical documents that will enhance your family history. Family Tree Maker makes it easy to add these directly from a website to your tree.

> Note: Before copying any images from the Web, make sure you aren't breaching any copyrights and/or get permission from the owner.

1 Click the **New Search** button.

2 Go to the Web page with the image you want to copy.

3 If you want to link the image to a different person, click the **Select a different person** button in the **Person From Your Tree** section at the bottom of the window. Select an individual and click **OK**.

4 Click the **Media** tab at the bottom of the workspace. On the Search Results Detail toolbar, click the **Enable web clipping** button.

5 Move the pointer over the Web page until the image you want is highlighted with a green dotted line.

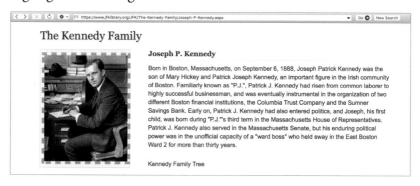

6   Click the highlighted image. A thumbnail of the image appears in the Search Results Detail section.

7   When you have selected all the images you want, click **Merge**. The Web Merge Wizard will launch.

8   Click **Merge**. A message tells you when the image has been added successfully. Click **OK** to close the message.

Note: The image will be linked to the person in the Person from Your Tree section. You can also view it on the Media workspace.

Copying Online Text to a Note

While surfing the Web, you may come upon interesting stories about a disaster that struck your grandfather's home town or a description of the ship your great-grandparents sailed to Australia on. You can easily save this type of information using the "Web clipping" tool.

1   Click the **New Search** button.

2   Go to the website you want to copy information from.

3   If you want to link the notes to a different person, click the **Select a different person** button in the Person from Your Tree section. Select an individual and click **OK**.

4   Click the **Notes** tab at the bottom of the workspace. To add the text as a personal note, click the **Person note** button on the Search Results Detail toolbar; to add the text as a research note, click the **Research note** button on the Search Results Detail toolbar.

5 On the Search Results Detail toolbar, click the **Enable web clipping** button.

6 Move the pointer over text on the website until the pointer turns into an I-beam. Highlight the text you want to copy. The **Insert Note** command appears.

7 Click **Insert Note**. The information now appears in the Search Results Detail section.

8 Click **Merge**. The Web Merge Wizard will launch.

9 Click **Merge**. A message tells you when the text has been added successfully. Click **OK** to close the message.

Note: The notes will be linked to the person in the Person from Your Tree section. To view the notes later, go to the individual's Person tab and click the Notes tab.

Archiving a Web Page

Websites are constantly changing and even disappearing. If you find a website you want to refer to multiple times, or if you find a site that contains too much information to read in one sitting, you might want to archive the Web page. That way, you can read the page's contents and continue your research when it's convenient for you—without being connected to the Internet. When you archive a Web page, Family Tree Maker will save a "snapshot" of the page in HTML format that can be opened in any Web browser.

1   Click the **New Search** button.

2   Go to the Web page you want to archive.

3   If you want to link the archived page to a different person, click the **Select a different person** button in the Person from Your Tree section. Select an individual and click **OK**.

4   Click the **Media** tab at the bottom of the workspace. In the Search Results Detail toolbar, click the **Create page archive** button.

A thumbnail of the page appears in the Search Results Detail section.

5   Click **Merge**. The Web Merge Wizard will launch.

6   Click **Merge**. A message tells you when the archived Web page has been added successfully. Click **OK** to close the message.

Note: The archived page will be linked to the person in the Person from Your Tree section. To view the archived page later, go to the Media workspace.

Managing Research Websites

You can create a list of favourite family history websites so they're easy to visit.

Adding a Website to Your Favourites List

1   Click the **Web Search** button on the main toolbar. In **Search Locations**, click the **New** button.

2   If you currently have the website open, click the **Use Current Site** button. If not, type the address for the website in the **URL Address** field.

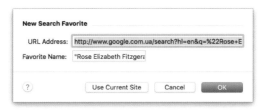

3   Type a title for the website in the **Favorite Name** field. This can be any name that helps you identify the website.

4   Click **OK**. The new website now appears in your list of favourites.

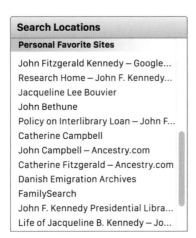

Sorting Your Website Favourites

If you've gathered quite a few favourite sites, you can sort the list so it appears in an order that's useful to you. For example, if you visit some websites daily, you can put them at the top of the list.

1   Click the **Web Search** button on the main toolbar. Click the **Manage Favorites** button at the bottom of the **Search Locations** area.

2   To display the websites in alphabetical order, select the **Sort favorites alphabetically** checkbox. To choose your own display order for the websites, deselect this checkbox, select a website and click the up and down arrows. When you've finished, click **OK**.

Part Three

Creating Charts, Reports, and Books

Chapter 9: Creating Family Tree Charts 145

Chapter 10: Running Reports 173

Chapter 11: Creating a Family History Book 201

Chapter Nine
Creating Family Tree Charts

After spending time gathering, compiling, and entering your family's history, it's time to show off your hard work. Family Tree Maker has a wide variety of family tree charts to help you bring your family history to life. Add your own personal touch by customising the charts with attractive backgrounds, colours, photos, fonts, and more. These charts help you quickly view the relationships between family members and are also a fun way to share your discoveries—hang a framed family tree in your home, print out multiple copies to share at a family reunion, or email charts to distant relatives.

As you begin creating your own charts, you might want to experiment with various formatting options, print out different versions, and see what you like best.

Pedigree Charts

The pedigree chart is a standard tool of genealogists and what most people think of when they hear the term "family tree". This chart shows the direct ancestors of one individual—parents, grandparents, great-grandparents, and so on.

Standard Pedigree Charts

In the standard pedigree chart (fig. 9-1), the primary individual is on the left side of the tree, with ancestors branching off to the right—paternal ancestors at the top and maternal ancestors at the bottom.

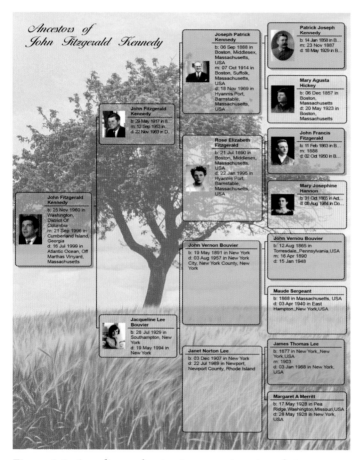

Figure 9-1. A pedigree chart using a custom template.

Vertical Pedigree Charts

In the vertical pedigree chart (fig. 9-2), the primary individual is shown at the bottom of the page, with his or her ancestors branching above the individual—paternal ancestors on the left and maternal ancestors on the right.

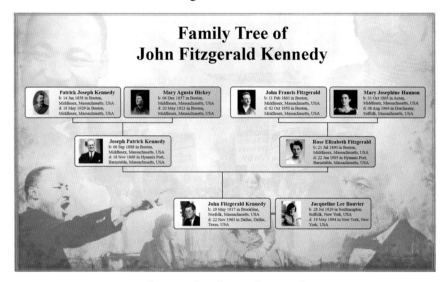

Figure 9-2. A customised vertical pedigree chart with images.

Hourglass Charts

An hourglass chart shows both the ancestors and descendants of an individual. The primary individual appears in the middle of the chart, with ancestors and descendants branching off in an hourglass or egg timer shape.

Note: Because of its shape and the number of individuals included, most hourglass charts look best as posters.

Standard Hourglass Charts

In the standard hourglass chart, the primary individual appears in the middle of the chart, with ancestors branching above and descendants extending below the person.

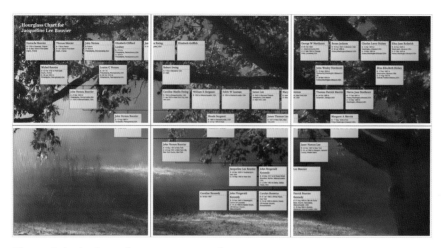

Figure 9-3. An hourglass poster spread over six pages.

The chart in figure 9-3 shows an hourglass chart laid out as a poster. Notice the white spaces running vertically and horizontally across the pages. These show the margins of a standard A4 sheet of paper. If you want to print the tree at home, you can use these guides to tape the pages together.

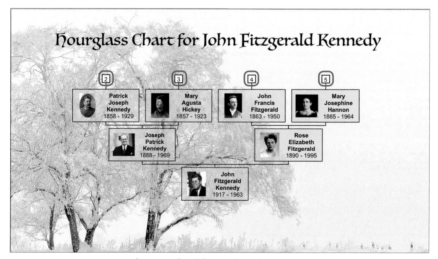

Figure 9-4. One page of a standard hourglass book chart.

You can also create standard hourglass charts that are useful for including in family history books. When you use the book layout, the chart is condensed into a series of individual family trees that appear on separate pages. The chart in figure 9-4 shows one page of a multi-page book chart. Notice the numbered boxes in the upper part of the chart. When you're viewing the chart in Family Tree Maker, you can click the box to access that page of the chart. And when your chart is printed, the numbered boxes help you navigate to related individuals found on other pages in the chart.

Horizontal Hourglass Charts

In the horizontal hourglass chart (fig. 9-5), the primary individual appears in the middle of the chart with ancestors branching to the right and descendants extending to the left of the person.

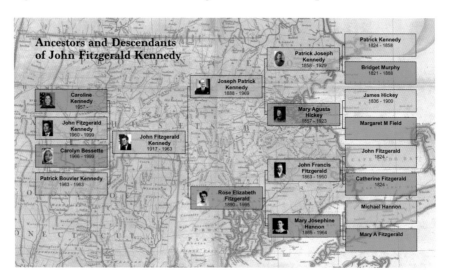

Figure 9-5. A horizontal hourglass chart.

Descendant Charts

The descendant chart shows the direct descendants of an individual—children, grandchildren, great-grandchildren, and so on. The primary individual is shown at the top of the chart, with descendants underneath in horizontal rows. You can also create a chart that shows the direct line between two selected individuals (fig. 9-6).

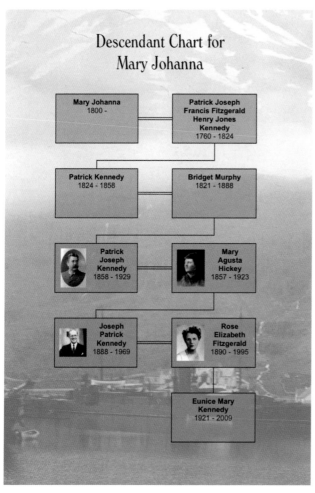

Figure 9-6. A direct-line descendant chart.

Bow Tie Charts

In the bow tie chart (fig. 9-7), the primary individual appears in the middle with paternal ancestors branching off to the left and maternal ancestors branching to the right.

Figure 9-7. A customised bow tie chart.

Family Tree Charts

In the family tree chart (fig. 9-8), the primary individual appears at the bottom of the chart, with ancestors branching above him or her in a tree shape.

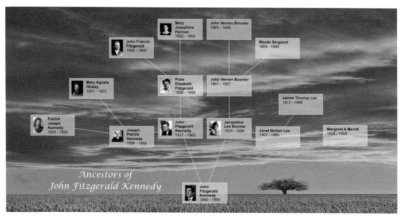

Figure 9-8. A customised family tree chart with images.

Fan Charts

A fan chart displays an individual's ancestors in a circular shape, one generation per level. The primary individual is at the centre or bottom of the chart. You can choose between a full circle, semi-circle (fig. 9-9), quarter-circle, and more.

Figure 9-9. A customised semi-circle fan chart.

> Note: Because of its shape and the number of individuals included, this chart is available only in poster layout.

Extended Family Charts

The extended family chart (fig. 9-10) can display every individual you've entered in your tree or just the people you select. The chart is arranged so that each generation appears on a separate horizontal row: children, parents, and grandparents, etc.

> Note: Because of its shape and the number of individuals included, this chart is available only in poster layout.

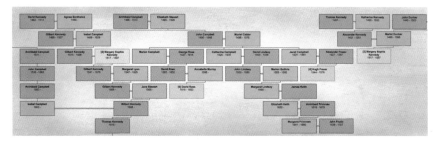

Figure 9-10. A section of an extended family chart.

Relationship Charts

The relationship chart (fig. 9-11) is a graphical representation of one person's relationship to another. The common relative is shown at the top of the chart, with direct-line ancestors and descendants shown vertically beneath the individual.

Figure 9-11. A relationship chart with a patterned background.

Creating a Chart

All charts are based on the last individual you were viewing in your tree. To change the primary individual in the chart, select an individual in the mini pedigree tree above the chart, or click the Index of Individuals button and select the person you want.

1   Go to the **Collection** tab on the Publish workspace. In **Publication Types**, select **Charts**.

2   Double-click the chart icon, or select its icon and click the **Detail** tab.

3   Use the editing panel to change the chart.

Customising a Chart

You can customise the contents and format of charts. For example, you can determine which facts are included and choose background images and fonts.

Note: You can save your custom changes as a template so you can use the same settings again. For instructions, see "Creating Your Own Template" on page 169.

Choosing Facts to Include in a Chart

In some charts you can choose which events or facts are included. Bear in mind that the more facts you add, the larger your chart will be.

1   Access the chart you want to change. In the editing toolbar, click the **Items to include** button.

The chart's default facts are shown in the Facts list. You can add and delete facts and change their display options.

2   Do one of the following:

- To delete a fact, select the fact and click the **Delete** (-) button.

- To add a fact, click the **Add** (+) button. The Select Fact dialog opens. Select a fact and click **OK**.

3   Change the fact options as necessary:

- **Include only preferred facts.** Select this checkbox to include only preferred facts. If you have multiple facts for the same event, only the preferred one is included.

- **Include private facts.** Select this checkbox to include facts you've marked as private.

- **Include blank facts.** Select this checkbox to include a fact label even if the fact is empty.

- **Display user-defined short place name.** Select this checkbox to use shortened place names for locations.

4 To change a fact's format, select the fact in the Facts list and click the **Options** button. Select the options you want, click **OK**.
Note: Options vary by fact. For example, you can include dates and locations in births, marriages, and deaths.

5 Select the **Print individual number with name** checkbox to assign numbers to individuals in the chart.

6 Click **OK** again.

Changing a Chart's Title

You can change the title that appears at the top of a chart. Access the chart you want to change. In the editing panel, type a new name in the **Chart title** field.

To reset the original chart title, click the button with a blue arrow on it.

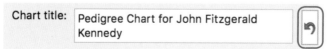

Including Source Information with a Chart

While you can't display sources in the actual chart, you can add a list of sources to the end of the chart (fig. 9-12).

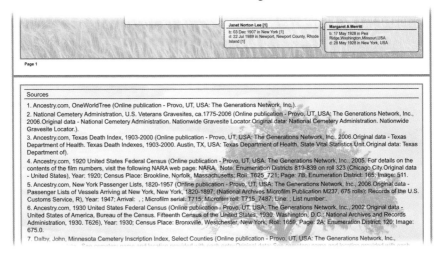

Figure 9-12. Sources on a pedigree chart.

1   Access the chart you want to change. In the editing toolbar, click the **Items to include** button.

2   Select the **Include sources** checkbox and click **OK**.

Adding Images and Texts to a Chart

You can personalise your charts and make them more appealing by adding backgrounds, family photographs, and portraits.

Adding a Background Image

Family Tree Maker comes with hundreds of attractive images you can use as chart backgrounds. Or you can create a background using an image from your computer or a photo from your tree.

1   Access the chart you want to change. In the editing panel, choose an image from the **Background** pop-up menu:

- To use an image from your computer, choose **Browse for an image**. Select an image and click **Open**.

- To use an image from your tree, choose **Select a media item**. Select an image and click **OK**.

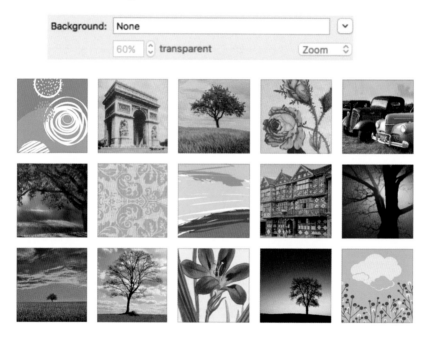

2   Choose how the background will be displayed. To centre the image on the page, choose **Center**. To stretch the image to fit the entire page, choose **Stretch**. To show a close-up of the image, choose **Zoom**. To show a series of the image, choose **Tile**.

3   Click the up and down arrows next to the **Transparent** percentage field to set the intensity of the image. You can also type an exact percentage directly in the field and press **Return**. At 0 percent, the image will look normal, while a higher percentage will fade the image so the chart is easier to read.

Adding Portraits to a Chart

You can include images of individuals in a chart. In order to do this, you must have already added the images to your tree and linked them to specific individuals. (For instructions, see "Adding a Portrait for an Individual" on page 95.)

1 Access the chart you want to change. Choose an image type from the **Pictures** pop-up menu:

   • Choose **Thumbnail** to use low-resolution thumbnail images.

   • Choose **Photo** to use the resolution of the actual photo.

2 From the pop-up menu, choose how images are positioned next to fact boxes:

   • To align images with the middle of boxes, choose **Center**.

   • To align images with the top of boxes, choose **Top**.

3 To change the size of the photo or thumbnail, type a size in the **Inches wide** field.

   Note: The larger the image is, the less space available for facts.

4 Select the **Use silhouettes** checkbox to display a silhouette icon for individuals who don't have portraits.

Adding a Decorative Photo or Embellishment

You can add family photographs, borders, or embellishments to your charts.

1 Access the chart you want to change. In the editing toolbar, click the **Insert Image or Text Box**  button.

2 Choose an image type from the pop-up menu:

- To use an image in your tree, choose **Insert Image from Media Collection**. Choose an image and click **OK**.

- To use an image on your computer, choose **Insert Image from File**. Choose an image and click **Open**.

- To use a graphic embellishment from the Family Tree Maker collection, choose **Insert Default Embellishment**. Choose an embellishment and click **Open**.

3 To resize an image, click it. Then move the pointer over the icon in the bottom-right corner. Click the corner and drag the image to the size you want.

4 To change the position of the image, move the pointer over the image, click it, and then drag the image to the location you want.

Adding Text

You can add text anywhere on a chart. For example, you could write a short biography of the main person in the chart (fig. 9-13).

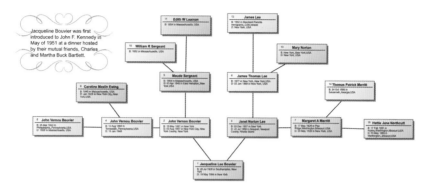

Figure 9-13. A family tree chart with a short biography.

1   Access the chart you want to add text to. In the editing toolbar, click the **Insert Image or Text Box** button.

2   Choose **Insert Text Box** from the pop-up menu.

3   To change the position of the text box, move the pointer over the text. When the pointer changes shape, click the box and drag it to the location you want.

4   To enter or edit text, double-click the box. Enter your text and click **OK**.

Tip: To change the text's size or colour, click the **Fonts** button in the charts toolbar. In "Items to format", select **Text Boxes**.

Changing the Header or Footer

You can define the headers and footers for each chart (the lines of text at the top and bottom of a chart).

1 Access the chart you want to change. In the editing toolbar, click the **Header/Footer** button.

2 Change the header and footer options as necessary:

- **Chart Note.** Type the text you want to appear in the footer.
- **Draw box around footer.** Select this checkbox to enclose the footer in a box.
- **Print "Created with Family Tree Maker."** Select this checkbox to add this statement to the footer.
- **Include submitter info.** Select this checkbox to add your user information to the footer. (To enter your user information, click **Tools > User Information**.)
- **Include date of printing.** Select this checkbox to include the current date in the footer.
- **Include time of printing.** Select this checkbox to include the current time in the footer.
- **Include page/chart numbers.** Select this checkbox to include page numbers. From the pop-up menu, choose whether the number appears in the header or footer.

  In **Starting number** type the number of the chart's first page; in **Starting number for continuation charts**, type the number of the second page of the chart.

3   Click **OK**.

Changing Formatting for a Chart

You can change a chart's formatting such as its fonts, colours and borders, and box sizes.

Changing Layout Options

Depending on the number of individuals and facts in your chart, you may need to adjust the layout and spacing to best display each individual.

Note: Not every option is available for every chart.

1   Access the chart you want to change. The editing panel displays the options you can change.

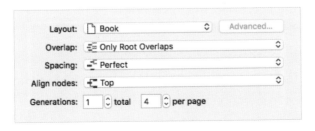

2   Change the chart's layout options as necessary:

- **Layout.** Choose **Book** to display the chart in pages suitable for using in a book; if a chart flows onto multiple pages, each page includes references to the generations continued on other pages. Choose **Poster** to display the chart in pages that can be linked together to form a poster (click the **Advanced** button to customise the poster format).

- **Overlap.** Determine the horizontal spacing of a chart. Choose **No Overlap** to space columns equally; choose **Columns Overlap** to overlap columns slightly; choose **Only Root Overlaps** to overlap the primary individual's column with the parents' column; choose **Fish Tail** to overlap all columns apart from the last generation.

- **Spacing.** Change the vertical spacing. Choose **Perfect** to space rows evenly; choose **Collapsed** to space rows closer together; choose **Squished** to use minimal space between rows; choose **Custom** to adjust the spacing using the Advanced poster format.

  Tip: Collapse or squish columns if you want to fit many people on one page.

- **Align nodes.** Choose how lines connect individuals. Choose **Top** to use lines underneath names; choose **Center** to centre lines next to each person; choose **Bezier** to use curved lines; choose **Straight** to use diagonal lines.

- **Center tree on page.** Select this checkbox to display the tree in the centre of the page. If the chart is for a book, don't use this option. Instead, leave extra space in the left margin for binding.

- **Last descendant generation vertically.** Select this checkbox to show the last generation under their parents.

- **Boxes overlap page breaks.** Select this checkbox so boxes that fall on a page break will be split over two pages.

- **Include empty branches.** In the Book layout, displays all branches of the tree through the generations you have specified even if there is no person entered for them.

  Printing empty branches is useful when you want to collect more information about your family. You can fill out the boxes by hand and later transfer the information to Family Tree Maker.

- **Include duplicate ancestor lines.** If you have an instance of intermarriage in your family (for example, cousins marrying back into the family), you will have some duplicate individuals in your tree. Select this option if you want these individuals to print in your tree more than once.

- **Include siblings of primary individual.** Displays the brothers and sisters of the person selected for the chart. Siblings are displayed on the same level as the primary person. This option is not available in the Book layout.

- **Include spouses of primary individual.** Displays each husband or wife of the person selected for the chart.

- **Include all individuals.** Includes everyone entered in the tree file in the chart, even those individuals who may not be attached to the main tree. These unrelated people are displayed in a separate tree (or trees) at the bottom of the chart. When this option is not selected, unrelated people do not appear in the chart.

- **Display relationship label for each node.** Shows each person's relationship to the person in the **Relation from** field.

- **Show generation labels.** Displays the relationship of the generation (parent, grandparent, and so forth) to the primary person above each column of the chart (excluding the root). The font and box style can be configured for all generation labels by clicking the **Fonts** and the **Box and Line Styles** buttons.

Note: You cannot move the generation labels. If you manually change the location of the columns, the labels may no longer be aligned.

- **Show thumbnail.** Displays the picture you assigned to each person that appears on the chart. If a picture is not available, a silhouette is displayed instead.

- **Include civil/canon information.** Displays the civil and canon degrees of separation at the bottom of the chart. For more information, see "Civil Degree" and "Canon Degree" in the Relationship Calculator section of Chapter 13 (page 242).

- **Root Node at Fan Origin.** Orients the primary person's box so that it is square with the page. In charts of 90 degrees or less, the primary person's node is placed in the bottom-left corner of the chart. When not selected, the root node is placed closer to the other nodes and oriented with the chart.

- **Fan layout.** Specifies the number of degrees to be used for the chart. The dark section of each circle indicates how the chart will appear.

Adding Page Borders, Text Boxes, and Background Colours

You can enhance a chart by adding a border, background colour, and text boxes.

1   Access the chart you want to change. In the editing toolbar, click the **Box and line styles** ☰ button.

2 To change the format of text boxes, select a group in the Boxes list.

3 Change these options as necessary:

-   Choose border, fill, and shadow colours from the pop-up menus.
-   Select **Double line** to add two lines to box borders.
-   Select **Rounded corners** to use round corners for box borders.
-   Select **All boxes same size** to make all boxes on the chart the same size.
-   Select **Semi-transparent** to make the background image or colour partially visible through boxes.
-   Select **Use gradient fill** to make a box's fill colour go from light to dark.

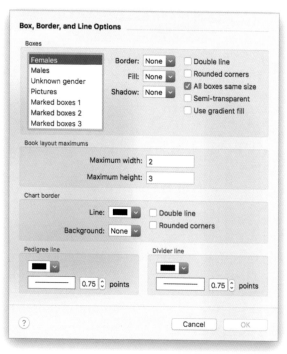

4   To change the size of boxes, type the maximum width and height (in inches) in "Poster layout initial box size".

5   To add a border to the entire chart, choose a colour from the **Line** pop-up menu. Then select **Double line** to add two lines to the page border; select **Rounded corners** to use round corners.

6   To add a coloured background, choose the colour from the **Background** pop-up menu. (Choose "None" for a blank background.)

7   To change the format of pedigree and divider lines, choose colours from the pop-up menus. Then choose the line thickness.

8   Click **OK**.

Changing Fonts

You can change the appearance of the text in charts to make it more formal, more fun, or maybe just more readable.

1   Access the chart you want to change. In the editing toolbar, click the **Fonts** button.

2   Select the text element, such as the chart title, you would like to change.

3   Choose a font from the **Font** pop-up menu. You can also change the size of the text, its style, colour, and alignment.

4   Click **OK**.

Using Chart Templates

Family Tree Maker comes with several templates you can use to quickly dress up your family tree charts. You can also turn your own chart designs into templates.

Creating Your Own Template

After you've customised a chart with your favourite fonts and colours and changed the spacing and layout to make everyone fit perfectly on the page, you don't want to lose your settings. You can save your modifications as a template, and you won't have to recreate your changes if you want to use them again on another chart.

1   After you've modified a chart, click the **Save settings**  button in the editing toolbar.

2   Select one of these options:
   •   **Save as preferred template.** This option saves the current settings as the preferred template for all charts. However, this template isn't permanent; if you modify the preferred template, the old settings will be written over.
   •   **Create new template.** This option lets you name the template and add it to the list of custom chart templates.

3   Click **Save**. To apply the template to another chart, see the next section.

Using a Custom Template

Family Tree Maker lets you use attractive templates to instantly change the look of your chart.

   You can apply a custom template to any chart. And if the results aren't exactly what you want, you can modify it.

1   Open the chart you want to apply a template to. In the editing toolbar, click the **Use saved settings**  button .

2   Select one of these template options:

- **Default.** This is the default chart template.
- **Preferred.** This is a template you have created and saved as your preferred template.
- **Custom.** These are the custom templates found in Family Tree Maker (and templates you have created).

3   Click **Use**.

Saving Charts

You can save a specific chart in Family Tree Maker, or you can save a chart in different file formats to export.

Saving a Specific Chart

If you like a chart you've created, you'll probably want to save it. That way you can view it again without having to recreate it.

1   Click the **Save chart**  button in the editing toolbar.

Pedigree Chart Options

2   Type a unique name for the chart. For example, don't use generic terms like "Pedigree Chart" or "Relationship Chart."

3   Click **Save**.

Tip: To open a saved chart, go to the Collection tab on the Publish workspace. In Publication Types, select **Saved Charts**. Then double-click the chart you want to open.

Saving a Chart as a File

You may want to save a chart as an image or PDF so you can share it easily with other family members or post it online.

1   Open the chart you want to save.

2   Click the **Share** button above the editing panel. From the pop-up menu, choose one of these commands:

   - **Export to PDF.** An Adobe PDF (Portable Document Format) is useful because it keeps the formatting you select. If you print a chart or send it to a relative, the chart will look exactly as you see it on your monitor. You cannot make changes to the PDF within Family Tree Maker.

   - **Export to One Page PDF.** This option exports the chart as one page (regardless of size). Use this option if you're creating a poster-sized chart or are going to have a chart professionaly printed.

   - **Export to Image.** This option lets you create an image of the chart as a bitmap or JPEG, or in another image format.

3   Select the location where you want to save the chart; then type a name for the chart and click **Save**.

Printing a Chart

1   Open the chart you want to print.

2   Click the **Print** button above the editing panel.

3   When prompted choose a printer, select the number of copies, and choose a page range.

4   Click **Print**.

Large Chart Printing

With Family Tree Maker, you can order a large, high-quality, professional print of your chart from the Family ChartMasters website in just a few clicks.

1   Open the chart you want to print.

2   Click the **Share** button above the editing panel, and then choose **Order Large Print at Family ChartMasters** from the pop-up menu.

3   In the message that appears, click **Export Chart to PDF**.

4   Change any options as necessary and click **Save**.

5   When the export process is complete, a new message appears. Click the **Go to Family ChartMasters Website** button.

6   The Family ChartMasters website opens in your default web browser. Follow the onscreen instructions to upload the exported file and order a large format print of your family tree.

Sharing a Chart

You can share your charts with others by emailing them as PDFs.

Note: You must be connected to the Internet and have a desktop email application to use this feature.

1   Access the chart you want to email.

2   Click the **Share** button above the editing panel. From the pop-up menu, choose **Send as PDF**.

3   Change any options as necessary and click **Save**. Family Tree Maker opens a new email with the file automatically attached in your default email application.

4   Send the email as you would any other.

Chapter Ten
Running Reports

Family Tree Maker includes a number of reports to help you organise and understand the information you've entered in your tree. You can create detailed reports about a single family, such as the family group sheet; relationship reports that show marriage events; bibliographies and source reports that help you keep track of your research; and more.

Each report can be customised—options differ by report. You can change fonts, add background images, and add headers and footers.

Genealogy Reports

Genealogy reports are a staple of serious family historians. These narrative reports contain biographical details about individuals. Relationships between people are shown using numbering systems that are unique to each report. You can choose from ancestor-ordered reports (Ahnentafels) or descendant-ordered reports.

Ahnentafel Report

The Ahnentafel (a German word meaning "ancestor table") is a numbered list of individuals (fig. 10-1). Its format is ancestor-ordered, meaning that it starts with one individual and moves backward in time to that individual's ancestors. This type of report isn't used frequently because it shows two family lines at the same time.

Ancestors of John Vernon Bouvier

Generation 1

1. **John Vernon Bouvier**, son of John Vernou Bouvier and Maude Sergeant was born on 19 May 1891 in New York, New York, USA. He died on 03 Aug 1957 in New York, New York, New York, USA. He married **Janet Norton Lee**. She was born on 03 Dec 1907 in New York, New York, USA. She died on 22 Jul 1989 in Newport, Newport County, Rhode Island, USA.

Generation 2

2. **John Vernou Bouvier**, son of John Vernou Bouvier and Caroline Maslin Ewing was born on 12 Aug 1865 in Torresdale, Philadelphia, Pennsylvania, USA. He died on 15 Jan 1948. He married **Maude Sergeant**, daughter of William R Sergeant and Edith W Leaman on 16 Apr 1890.

3. **Maude Sergeant**, daughter of William R Sergeant and Edith W Leaman was born in 1868 in Massachusetts, USA. She died on 03 Apr 1940 in East Hampton, Suffolk, New York, USA.

Maude Sergeant and John Vernou Bouvier had the following child:

Figure 10-1. An Ahnentafel (ancestor report).

Descendant Report

A descendant report (fig. 10-2) is a narrative report that includes biographical information about each individual. It is descendant-ordered, meaning it starts with an individual and moves forward in time through that individual's children and grandchildren. There are four numbering system options: Register, NGSQ, Henry, and d'Aboville.

Descendants of John Vernon Bouvier

Generation 1

1. **JOHN VERNON[1] BOUVIER** was born on 19 May 1891 in New York. He died on 03 Aug 1957 in New York City, New York County, New York. He married **JANET NORTON LEE**. She was born on 03 Dec 1907 in New York. She died on 22 Jul 1989 in Newport, Newport County, Rhode Island.

John Vernon Bouvier and Janet Norton Lee had the following children:

2. i. JACQUELINE LEE[2] BOUVIER was born on 28 Nov 1929 in Southampton, New York. She died on 19 May 1994 in New York. She married (1) JOHN FITZGERALD KENNEDY, son of Joseph Patrick Kennedy and Rose Elizabeth Fitzgerald on 12 Sep 1953 in Newport, Newport, Rhode Island, USA (The couple were married on September 12, 1953 at St. Mary's Church in Newport, Rhode Island. The 11 a.m. ceremony was officiated by Archbishop Richard Cushing. A whopping 750 guests attended, with an additional 3,000 well-wishers who waited outside). He was born on 29 May 1917 in Brookline, Norfolk, Massachusetts, USA (Kennedy was born at 83 Beals Street in Brookline, Massachusetts on Tuesday, May 29, 1917, at 3:00 p.m.). He died on 22 Nov 1963 in Dallas, Dallas, Texas, USA. She married PRETEND SPOUSE.

Figure 10-2. A Register descendant report.

Person Reports

Person reports give you an overview of your tree and help you focus on specific individuals.

Custom Report

Custom reports (fig. 10-3) let you explore your tree in ways that are interesting to you. For example, you can create a custom report of birthplaces or causes of death.

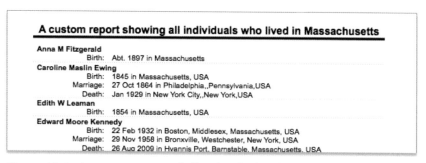

Figure 10-3. A custom report of all individuals who lived in Massachusetts.

Data Errors Report

The Data Errors Report (fig. 10-4) lists all instances where data is missing or may be incorrect. This includes nonsensical dates (e.g., an individual being born before his or her parents were born), empty fields, and duplicate individuals. (For more information, see "Running the Data Errors Report" on page 270.)

Data Errors Report

Name	Birth Date	Potential Error
Lee Bouvier		The birth date is missing.
Muriel Calder	13 Feb 1498	The marriage date is missing.
Catherine Fitzgerald	Abt. 1824	The marriage date is missing. The individual has the same last name as his/her spouse, John Fitzgerald.
John Fitzgerald	Abt. 1824	The individual has the same last

Figure 10-4. A Data Errors Report.

Individual Report

The Individual Report (fig. 10-5) lists every fact and source you have recorded for a specific individual.

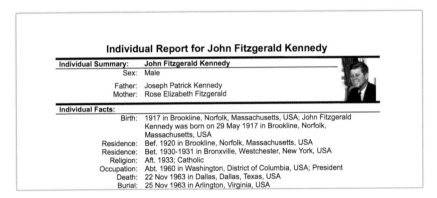

Figure 10-5. An Individual Report.

LDS Ordinances Report

The LDS Ordinances Report (fig. 10-6) is useful for members of The Church of Jesus Christ of Latter-day Saints and displays LDS-specific ordinances such as baptisms and sealings.

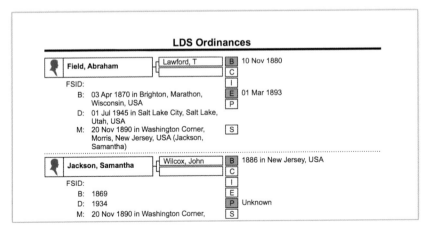

Figure 10-6. An LDS Ordinances Report.

LDS Ordinance Summary Report

The LDS Ordinance Summary Report (fig. 10-7) lists all people in the tree and their LDS ordinances status. You can restrict the report to selected individuals.

LDS Ordinance Summary

Name	Lifespan	Spouse	B	C	I	E	P	S
Field, Abraham	1870 - 1945	Jackson, Samantha	X			X		
Jackson, Samantha	1869 - 1934	Field, Abraham	X				X	
Lawford, Thomas	1851 - Unknown			X				
Smith, Herbert	Unknown - Unknown	Steward, Phoebe Jackson	X					
Steward, Phoebe Jackson	1900 - 1948	Smith, Herbert				X		

Figure 10-7. An LDS Ordinance Summary Report.

Note: Choose **Family Tree Maker 2017>Preferences** and then select the **Show LDS information** checkbox to access the LDS Ordinances Report and the LDS Ordinance Summary Report.

List of Individuals Report

The List of Individuals Report has five options: all individuals in your tree, all individuals and their ID numbers, a list of anniversaries, a list of birthdays (fig. 10-8), and a contact list.

Birthday List

Name	Birth	Birthday	Death	Age
Bessette, Carolyn	07 Jan 1966	53	16 Jul 1999	33
Kennedy, Patrick Joseph	14 Jan 1858	161	18 May 1929	71
Bouvier, Michel	02 Feb 1792	227	09 Jun 1874	82
Fitzgerald, John Francis	11 Feb 1863	155	02 Oct 1950	87
Calder, Muriel	13 Feb 1498	520	1575	76

Figure 10-8. A list of birthdays.

Notes Report

The Notes Report (fig. 10-9) lets you view the person, research, relationship, or fact notes you've entered in your tree.

Notes Report	
Kennedy, John Fitzgerald	**1917 - 22 Nov 1963**
Person Note:	In September 1935, Kennedy made his first trip abroad when he traveled to London with his parents and his sister Kathleen. He intended to study under Harold Laski at the London School of Economics (LSE), as his older brother had done. Ill-health forced his return to America in October of that year, when he enrolled late and spent six weeks at Princeton University. He was then hospitalized for observation at Peter Bent Brigham Hospital in Boston.
NameFact Note:	John Fitzgerald Kennedy was named in honor of Rose's father, John Francis Fitzgerald, the Boston Mayor popularly known as Honey Fitz. Before long, family and friends called this small blue-eyed baby, Jack.
Kennedy, Joseph Patrick	**06 Sep 1888 - 18 Nov 1969**
Research Note:	The couple had nine children. As Kennedy's business expanded, he

Figure 10-9. A report of several notes.

Surname Report

The Surname Report (fig. 10-10) lists the total number of individuals with a specific surname, the number of males and females with that surname, and the earliest and most recent year a surname appears in your tree.

Surname Report

Surname	Count	Male	Female	Earliest	Most recent
Kennedy	20	14	6	1517	1963
Lawford	1	1	0	1923	1923
Leaman	1	0	1	1854	1854
Lee	3	2	1	1852	1907
Lindsay	6	3	3	1503	1772
Lyon	1	0	1	1547	1547
Maslin	1	1	0	1770	1770
Mercier	1	0	1	1766	1766
Merritt	2	1	1	1878	1885
Murphy	1	0	1	1821	1821
Murray	1	0	1	1586	1586

Figure 10-10. A Surname Report sorted by name count.

Task List

A task list (fig. 10-11) shows all the research tasks on your to-do list. You can see each task's priority, category, and creation and due dates.

Task List

Status	Task Information	Date Due
☐ !	Scan photos for mom's personal history Task for: General Task Categories: Created: 2/10/18	2/16/18
☐ !	Write to Berks Country Historical Society for Reed/Rieth church records Task for: General Task Categories: Reed Created: 2/10/18	2/13/18
☐ –	Look for marriage record for Joseph Thompson and "Jane" between 1840 and 1845 in Warwickshire, England Task for: General Task Categories: Thompson Created: 2/10/18	3/10/18

Figure 10-11. A research to-do list.

Timeline Report

A timeline (fig. 10-12) lists an individual's life events with the date and location of the event and the person's age at the time. You can also include events for an individual's immediate family (such as birth, marriage, and death) and historical events.

Timeline Report for Joseph Patrick Kennedy

Yr/Age	Event	Date/Place/Description
1888	Birth	06 Sep 1888 Boston, Middlesex, Massachusetts, USA
1890	Birth (spouse) Rose Elizabeth Fitzgerald	21 Jul 1890 Boston, Middlesex, Massachusetts, USA
1891 2	Birth (brother) Francis Kennedy	11 Mar 1891
1892 3	Death (brother) Francis Kennedy	14 Jan 1892
1892 3	Birth (sister) Loretta Kennedy	06 Aug 1892
1898 10	Birth (sister) Margaret Kennedy	22 Oct 1898

Figure 10-12. A timeline for an individual and his family.

Relationship Reports

Relationship reports are just what they sound like; they show the relationships between different individuals and families in your tree.

Family Group Sheet

A family group sheet (fig. 10-13) is one of the most commonly used reports in the area of family history. It is a detailed report about a single family (primarily the parents and children of a family, although it also includes the names of the couple's parents). It includes names; birth, death, and marriage information; notes; and sources. If the individual has more than one spouse, additional family group sheets will be created for each family.

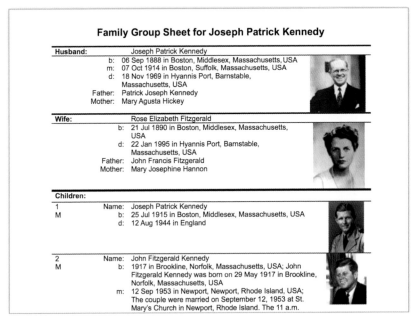

Family Group Sheet for Joseph Patrick Kennedy

Husband:	Joseph Patrick Kennedy
b:	06 Sep 1888 in Boston, Middlesex, Massachusetts, USA
m:	07 Oct 1914 in Boston, Suffolk, Massachusetts, USA
d:	18 Nov 1969 in Hyannis Port, Barnstable, Massachusetts, USA
Father:	Patrick Joseph Kennedy
Mother:	Mary Agusta Hickey

Wife:	Rose Elizabeth Fitzgerald
b:	21 Jul 1890 in Boston, Middlesex, Massachusetts, USA
d:	22 Jan 1995 in Hyannis Port, Barnstable, Massachusetts, USA
Father:	John Francis Fitzgerald
Mother:	Mary Josephine Hannon

Children:

1 M	Name:	Joseph Patrick Kennedy
	b:	25 Jul 1915 in Boston, Middlesex, Massachusetts, USA
	d:	12 Aug 1944 in England

2 M	Name:	John Fitzgerald Kennedy
	b:	1917 in Brookline, Norfolk, Massachusetts, USA; John Fitzgerald Kennedy was born on 29 May 1917 in Brookline, Norfolk, Massachusetts, USA
	m:	12 Sep 1953 in Newport, Newport, Rhode Island, USA; The couple were married on September 12, 1953 at St. Mary's Church in Newport, Rhode Island. The 11 a.m.

Figure 10-13. A family group sheet.

Kinship Report

The Kinship Report (fig. 10-14) helps you determine how individuals in your tree are related to a specific person.

Kinship Report for Joseph Patrick Kennedy

Name:	Birth Date:	Relationship:
Kennedy, Joseph Patrick	06 Sep 1888	Self
Kennedy, John	1715	3rd great grandfather
Kennedy, Kathleen "Kick" Agnes	20 Feb 1920	Daughter
Kennedy, Patricia	06 May 1924	Daughter
Kennedy, Rosemary	13 Sep 1918	Daughter
Kennedy, Patrick Joseph	14 Jan 1858	Father
Kennedy, Kara Anne	27 Feb 1960	Granddaughter
Kennedy, John Fitzgerald	25 Nov 1960	Grandson
Kennedy, Michael LeMoyne	27 Feb 1958	Grandson
Kennedy, Patrick Bouvier	07 Aug 1963	Grandson
Kennedy, Patrick Joseph Francis Fitzgerald Henry Jones	1760	Great grandfather

Figure 10-14. A Kinship Report.

Marriage Report

The Marriage Report (fig. 10-15) shows husbands and wives, their marriage dates, and relationship statuses.

Marriage Report

Husband:	Wife:	Marriage Date:	Relation:
Bouvier, Eustache	Mercier, Therese	03 Feb 1789	Spouse - Ongoing
Bouvier, John Vernon	Lee, Janet Norton		Spouse - Ongoing
Bouvier, John Vernou	Sergeant, Maude	16 Apr 1890	Spouse - Ongoing
Bouvier, John Vernou	Ewing, Caroline Maslin	27 Oct 1864	Spouse - Ongoing
Bouvier, Michel	Vernou, Louise C	29 May 1828	Spouse - Ongoing
Fitzgerald, John	Fitzgerald, Catherine		Spouse - Ongoing
Fitzgerald, John Francis	Hannon, Mary Josephine	1888	Spouse - Ongoing
Hulsey, Charles Leroy	Roderick, Eliza Jane	31 Jul 1856	Spouse - Ongoing
Kennedy, John Fitzgerald	Bouvier, Jacqueline Lee	12 Sep 1953	Spouse - Ongoing
Kennedy, John Fitzgerald	Bessette, Carolyn	21 Sep 1996	Spouse - Ongoing
Kennedy, Joseph Patrick	Fitzgerald, Rose Elizabeth	07 Oct 1914	Spouse - Ongoing

Figure 10-15. A Marriage Report.

Outline Ancestor Report

The Outline Ancestor Report (fig. 10-16) shows where everyone fits in the family. Starting with a relative, it moves into the past, showing the primary individual's parents, grandparents, great-grandparents, and so on, generation by generation in outline format, with each individual on a separate line.

Outline Ancestor Report for Joseph Patrick Kennedy

1   Joseph Patrick Kennedy b: 06 Sep 1888 in Boston, Middlesex, Massachusetts, USA, d: 18 Nov
     1969 in Hyannis Port, Barnstable, Massachusetts, USA
  + Rose Elizabeth Fitzgerald b: 21 Jul 1890 in Boston, Middlesex, Massachusetts, USA, m: 07
     Oct 1914 in Boston, Suffolk, Massachusetts, USA, d: 22 Jan 1995 in Hyannis Port,
     Barnstable, Massachusetts, USA
...2 Patrick Joseph Kennedy b: 14 Jan 1858 in Boston, Middlesex, Massachusetts, USA, d: 18
     May 1929 in Boston, Middlesex, Massachusetts, USA
  + Mary Agusta Hickey b: 06 Dec 1857 in Boston, Middlesex, Massachusetts, USA, m: 23 Nov
     1887, d: 20 May 1923 in Boston, Middlesex, Massachusetts, USA
......3 Patrick Kennedy b: 1824 in Ireland, d: 22 Nov 1858 in Boston, Middlesex, Massachusetts,
     USA

Figure 10-16. An Outline Ancestor Report.

Outline Descendant Report

The Outline Descendant Report (fig. 10-17) starts with an ancestor and outlines each generation of descendants; you can choose the number of generations to show in the report.

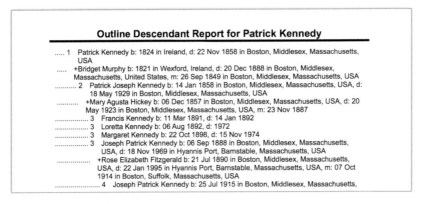

Outline Descendant Report for Patrick Kennedy

..... 1 Patrick Kennedy b: 1824 in Ireland, d: 22 Nov 1858 in Boston, Middlesex, Massachusetts,
     USA
..... +Bridget Murphy b: 1821 in Wexford, Ireland, d: 20 Dec 1888 in Boston, Middlesex,
     Massachusetts, United States, m: 26 Sep 1849 in Boston, Middlesex, Massachusetts, USA
..........2 Patrick Joseph Kennedy b: 14 Jan 1858 in Boston, Middlesex, Massachusetts, USA, d:
     18 May 1929 in Boston, Middlesex, Massachusetts, USA
.... +Mary Agusta Hickey b: 06 Dec 1857 in Boston, Middlesex, Massachusetts, USA, d: 20
     May 1923 in Boston, Middlesex, Massachusetts, USA, m: 23 Nov 1887
...............3 Francis Kennedy b: 11 Mar 1891, d: 14 Jan 1892
...............3 Loretta Kennedy b: 06 Aug 1892, d: 1972
...............3 Margaret Kennedy b: 22 Oct 1898, d: 15 Nov 1974
...............3 Joseph Patrick Kennedy b: 06 Sep 1888 in Boston, Middlesex, Massachusetts,
     USA, d: 18 Nov 1969 in Hyannis Port, Barnstable, Massachusetts, USA
.... +Rose Elizabeth Fitzgerald b: 21 Jul 1890 in Boston, Middlesex, Massachusetts,
     USA, d: 22 Jan 1995 in Hyannis Port, Barnstable, Massachusetts, USA, m: 07 Oct
     1914 in Boston, Suffolk, Massachusetts, USA
.....................4 Joseph Patrick Kennedy b: 25 Jul 1915 in Boston, Middlesex, Massachusetts,

Figure 10-17. An Outline Descendant Report.

Parentage Report

The Parentage Report (fig. 10-18) lists each individual, his or her parents, and their relationship (e.g., biological, adopted, foster).

Parentage Report

Name	Parents	Relationship
Kennedy, Loretta	Kennedy, Patrick Joseph	Biological
	Hickey, Mary Agusta	Biological
Kennedy, Margaret	Kennedy, Patrick Joseph	Biological
	Hickey, Mary Agusta	Biological
Kennedy, Francis	Kennedy, Patrick Joseph	Biological
	Hickey, Mary Agusta	Biological
Hickey, Mary Agusta	Hickey, James	Biological
	Field, Margaret M	Biological

Figure 10-18. A Parentage Report.

Family View Report

The Family View Report (fig. 10-19) shows three generations of ancestors for an individual and his or her parents and children.

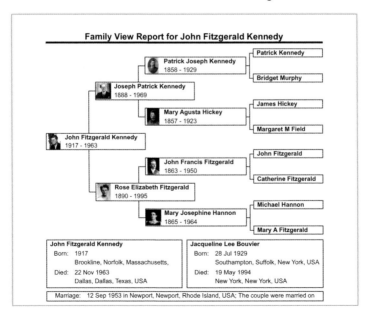

Figure 10-19. A Family View Report.

Place Usage Report

The Place Usage Report (fig. 10-20) lists the locations in your tree and each person associated with them. You can also include specific events, such as birth or marriage, that occurred at that location.

Place Usage Report

Arlington, Virginia, USA
Kennedy, John Fitzgerald
    Burial: 25 Nov 1963
Atlantic Ocean, Off Marthas Vinyard, Massachusetts, USA
Kennedy, John Fitzgerald
    Death: 16 Jul 1999
Boston City, Suffolk, Massachusetts
Fitzgerald, Rose Elizabeth
    Res: 1900
    Res: 1900
Boston, Middlesex, Massachusetts, USA
Fitzgerald, Rose Elizabeth
    Birth: 21 Jul 1890
Kennedy, Edward Moore
    Birth: 22 Feb 1932

Figure 10-20. A Place Usage Report.

Media Reports

Media reports let you view items individually or in groups.

Photo Album

A photo album (fig. 10-21) shows a person's birth and death dates, the names of their parents, and all photos linked to them.

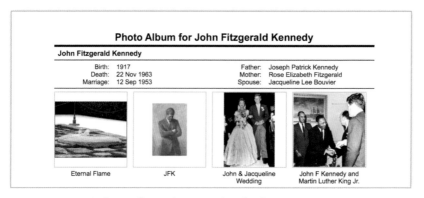

Figure 10-21. A photo album for an individual.

Media Item Report

A Media Item Report (fig. 10-22) shows an image (or icon) of a media item, its caption, date of origin, description, and individuals linked to the item.

Media Item

Caption: The Kennedy Family at
            Hyannis Port 1931
Date: 09/04/1931
Categories: Photos

Description: The Kennedy Family at Hyannis Port, 04
             September 1931. L-R: Robert Kennedy, John
             F. Kennedy, Eunice Kennedy, Jean Kennedy
             (on lap of) Joseph P. Kennedy Sr., Rose
             Fitzgerald Kennedy (behind) Patricia Kennedy,
             Kathleen Kennedy, Joseph P. Kennedy Jr.
             (behind) Rosemary Kennedy.

Links:

Person: Robert Kennedy
Person: John F. Kennedy
Person: Eunice Kennedy
Person: Jean Kennedy
Person: Joseph P. Kennedy Sr.
Person: Rose Fitzgerald Kennedy
Person: Patricia Kennedy
Person: Kathleen Kennedy
Person: Joseph P. Kennedy Jr.

Figure 10-22. A Media Item Report.

Media Usage Report

The Media Usage Report (fig. 10-23) lists all your media items. For each item you'll see a thumbnail, name, location on your computer, and sources the item is linked to.

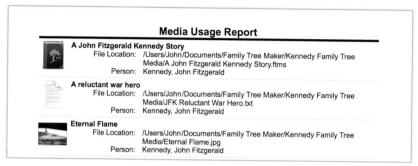

Figure 10-23. A Media Usage Report.

Source Reports

Family Tree Maker includes several reports that help you see how you've sourced facts in your tree.

Bibliography

A bibliography (fig. 10-24) is a detailed list of all the sources used in your research.

Source Bibliography

Ancestry Family Trees (Online publication - Provo, UT, USA: The Generations Network. Original data: Family Tree files submitted by Ancestry members.).

Ancestry.com and The Church of Jesus Christ of Latter-day Saints, 1880 United States Federal Census (Online publication - Provo, UT, USA: The Generations Network, Inc., 2005. 1880 U.S. Census Index provided by The Church of Jesus Christ of Latter-day Saints © Copyright 1999 Intellectual Reserve, Inc. All rights reserved. All use is subject to the limite).

Ancestry.com, 1860 United States Federal Census (Online publication - Provo, UT, USA: The Generations Network, Inc., 2004.Original data - United States of America, Bureau of the Census. Eighth Census of the United States, 1860. Washington, D.C.: National Archives and Records Administration, 1860. M653, 1).

Figure 10-24. An annotated bibliography.

Documented Facts Report

The Documented Facts Report (fig. 10-25) shows an individual and the events you've entered source information for.

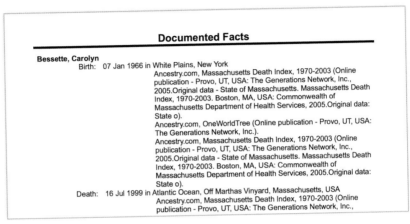

Documented Facts

Bessette, Carolyn
Birth: 07 Jan 1966 in White Plains, New York
Ancestry.com, Massachusetts Death Index, 1970-2003 (Online publication - Provo, UT, USA: The Generations Network, Inc., 2005.Original data - State of Massachusetts. Massachusetts Death Index, 1970-2003. Boston, MA, USA: Commonwealth of Massachusetts Department of Health Services, 2005.Original data: State o).
Ancestry.com, OneWorldTree (Online publication - Provo, UT, USA: The Generations Network, Inc.).
Ancestry.com, Massachusetts Death Index, 1970-2003 (Online publication - Provo, UT, USA: The Generations Network, Inc., 2005.Original data - State of Massachusetts. Massachusetts Death Index, 1970-2003. Boston, MA, USA: Commonwealth of Massachusetts Department of Health Services, 2005.Original data: State o).
Death: 16 Jul 1999 in Atlantic Ocean, Off Marthas Vinyard, Massachusetts, USA
Ancestry.com, Massachusetts Death Index, 1970-2003 (Online publication - Provo, UT, USA: The Generations Network, Inc.,

Figure 10-25. A Documented Facts Report.

Undocumented Facts Report

The Undocumented Facts Report (fig. 10-26) shows individuals and events that don't have sources associated with them.

Undocumented Facts

Bennett, Virginia Joan
Marr: (Edward Moore Kennedy) 29 Nov 1958 in Bronxville, Westchester, New York, USA
Name: Bennett, Virginia Joan
Sex: Female
Bessette, Carolyn
Marr: (John Fitzgerald Kennedy) 21 Sep 1996 in Cumberland Island, Georgia
Sex: Female
Bouvier, Jacqueline Lee
Engage: (John Fitzgerald Kennedy) 24 Jun 1953 in Brookline, Norfolk, Massachusetts, USA; John proposed to Jackie with a Van Cleef and Arpels engagement ring that his father helped him pick. The ring consisted of a 2.88 carat diamond and 2.84 carat emerald with tapering baguettes.
Grad: 1947 in New York, New York, USA; Vassar College
Sex: Female

Figure 10-26. An Undocumented Facts Report.

Source Usage Report

The Source Usage Report (fig. 10-27) shows each source and the individuals and facts associated with it.

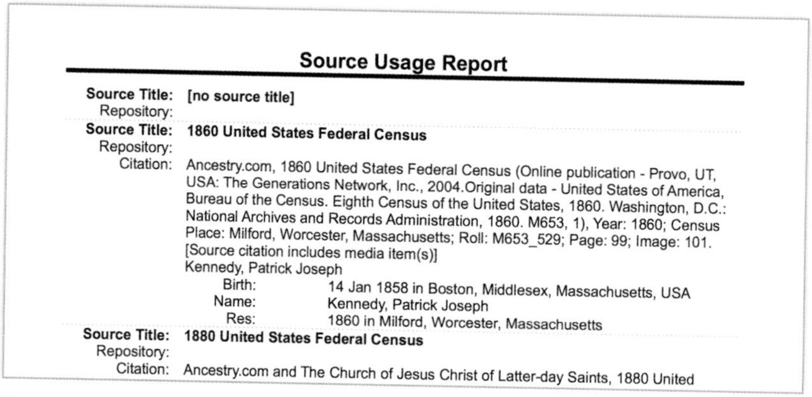

Source Usage Report

Source Title: **[no source title]**
Repository:
Source Title: **1860 United States Federal Census**
Repository:
Citation: Ancestry.com, 1860 United States Federal Census (Online publication - Provo, UT, USA: The Generations Network, Inc., 2004.Original data - United States of America, Bureau of the Census. Eighth Census of the United States, 1860. Washington, D.C.: National Archives and Records Administration, 1860. M653, 1), Year: 1860; Census Place: Milford, Worcester, Massachusetts; Roll: M653_529; Page: 99; Image: 101. [Source citation includes media item(s)]
Kennedy, Patrick Joseph
Birth: 14 Jan 1858 in Boston, Middlesex, Massachusetts, USA
Name: Kennedy, Patrick Joseph
Res: 1860 in Milford, Worcester, Massachusetts
Source Title: **1880 United States Federal Census**
Repository:
Citation: Ancestry.com and The Church of Jesus Christ of Latter-day Saints, 1880 United

Figure 10-27. A Source Usage Report.

Calendars

You can make calendars (fig. 10-28) that display birthdays, death dates, and anniversaries for your immediate family or ancestors.

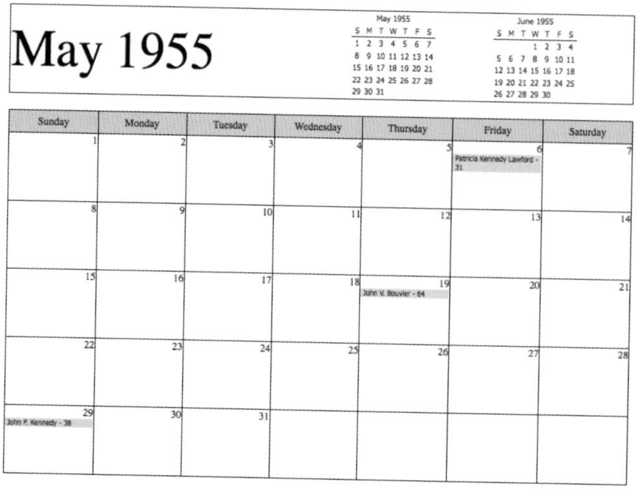

Figure 10-28. A calendar showing birth dates for all individuals.

Creating a Report

All reports are based on the last individual you were viewing in your tree. To change the primary individual in the report, select an individual in the mini pedigree tree above the report, or click the Index of Individuals button and select the person you want.

1 Go to the **Collection** tab on the Publish workspace. In **Publication Types**, select the report type you want.

2 Double-click the report icon, or select its icon and click the **Detail** tab.

3 Use the editing panel to change the report.

Customising a Report

You can customise the contents and format of reports. For example, you can determine which individuals and facts are included in the report and choose background images and fonts.

Choosing Facts to Include in a Report

In some reports you can decide which events or facts you'd like to include.

1 Access the report you want to change. In the editing toolbar, click the **Items to include** button.

The Items to Include dialog opens. The report's default facts are shown in the Facts list. You can add and delete facts and also change their display options.

2 Do one of the following:

- To delete a fact, select the fact and click the **Delete** (-) button.

- To add a fact, click the **Add** (+) button. The Select Fact dialog opens. Select a fact and click **OK**.

3 Change the fact options as necessary:

- **Include only preferred facts.** Select this checkbox to include only preferred facts. If you have multiple facts for the same event, only the preferred one is included.

- **Include private facts.** Select this checkbox to include facts you've marked as private.

- **Include blank facts.** Select this checkbox to include a fact label even if the fact is empty.

- **Display user-defined short place name.** Select this check-box to use shortened place names for locations.

4 To change a fact's format, select the fact in the Facts list and click the **Options** button. Select the options you want and click **OK**.

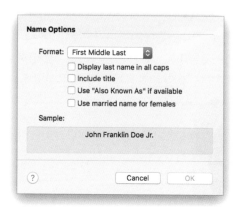

Note: The options vary by fact. For example, you can include dates and locations in births, marriages, and deaths.

5 Choose notes to include in the report:

- Select **Include person notes** to show person notes linked to individuals.

- Select **Include research notes** to show research notes linked to individuals.

- Select **Include relationship notes** to show person notes linked to relationships.

- Select **Include fact notes** to show notes linked to facts.

- Select **Include private notes** to show a note even if it has been marked as private.

6   To show sources in the report, select the **Include sources** checkbox.

7   Click **OK**.

Choosing Individuals to Include in a Report

In many reports, you can choose which individuals will be included. For example, you can choose a specific ancestor and his or her descendants. You can also choose individuals by picking specific criteria (for example, you may want to create a report that shows all individuals who were born in a particular city).

1   Access the report you want to change. You can select individuals for the report in the editing panel.

2   Do one of the following:

  • To include the individual's children, spouses, and parents, select **Immediate family**.

  • To also include grandparents, aunts, uncles, first cousins, nieces, nephews, grandchildren, and spouses of all those who are listed, select **Extended family**.

  • To include everyone in your tree, select **All individuals**.

  • To choose specific individuals, select **Selected individuals**. The Filter Individuals dialog opens. Select a name and then click **Include** to add the person. When you've finished choosing individuals, click **OK**.

Changing a Report's Title

You can change the title that appears at the top of a report. Access the report you want to change. In the editing panel, type a new name in the **Report title** field.

Adding a Background Image

Family Tree Maker comes with hundreds of attractive images you can use as report backgrounds. Or you can create a background using an image from your computer or a photo from your tree.

1   Access the report you want to change. In the editing panel, choose an image from the **Background** pop-up menu:

   •   To use an image from your computer, choose **Browse for an image**. Select an image and click **Open**.

   •   To use an image from your tree, choose **Select a media item**. Select an image and click **OK**.

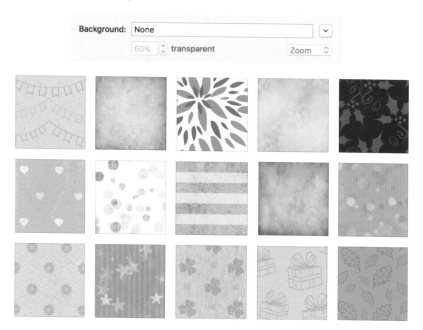

2   Determine how the background will be displayed. To centre the image on the page, choose **Center**. To stretch the image to fit the entire page, choose **Stretch**. To show a close-up of the image, choose **Zoom**. To show a series of the image, choose **Tile**.

3   Click the up and down arrows next to the **Transparent** percentage field to set the intensity of the image. You can also type an exact percentage directly in the field and press Return. At 0 percent, the image will look normal, while a higher percentage will fade the image so the report is easier to read.

Changing the Header or Footer

You can define a report's headers and footers (the lines of text at the top and bottom of the page).

1   Access the report you want to change. In the editing toolbar, click the **Header/Footer** button.

2   Change the header and footer options as necessary:

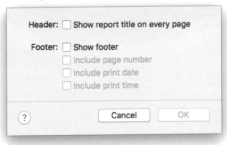

- **Show report title on every page.** Select this checkbox to display a header (the title) on each page of the report.

- **Show footer.** Select this checkbox to display a footer on each page of the report. Select **Include page number** to display a page number on the left side of the footer; select **Include print date** to display the current date on the right side of the footer; select **Include print time** to display the current time next to the current date.

3 Click **OK**.

Changing Fonts

You can change the appearance of the text in reports to make it more formal, more fun, or maybe just more readable.

1 Access the report you want to change. In the editing toolbar, click the **Fonts Aa** button.

2 Select the text element, such as the report title, you want to change.

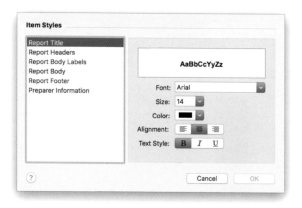

3 Choose a font from the **Font** pop-up menu. You can also change the size of the font, its style, colour, and alignment.

4 Click **OK**.

Saving Reports

You can save a specific report in Family Tree Maker, or you can save a report in different file formats to export.

Saving the Settings for a Report

After you've customised a report, you can save your settings so you won't have to recreate these changes the next time you want to view the report. The settings you can save depend on the report, but generally include fact options, fonts, headers and footers, page layouts, and background images.

Note: You cannot save settings in one report and use them in another. For example, if you save settings in the Parentage Report, you cannot use the same settings in the Kinship Report.

1   After you've modified a report, click the **Save settings**

button in the editing toolbar.

2   A message asks if you want to use the current settings as the preferred settings for this report type. Click **OK**.

Tip: To change back to the report's default settings, click the **Use report settings** button in the editing toolbar. Then select **Default settings** and click **OK**.

Saving a Specific Report

If you like a report you've created, you'll probably want to save it. That way you can view it again without having to recreate it.

1 After you've modified a report, click the **Save report**  button in the editing toolbar.

2 Type a unique name for the report. For example, don't use generic terms like "Family Group Sheet" or "Custom Report".

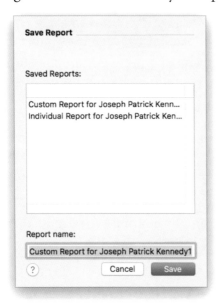

3 Click **Save**.

Tip: To open a saved report, go to the Collection tab on the Publish workspace. In Publication Types, select **Saved Reports**. Then double-click the report you want to open.

Saving a Report as a File

You may want to save a report as a document or spreadsheet so you can share it easily with other family members or post it online.

1   Access the report you want to save.

2   Click the **Share** button above the editing panel. From the pop-up menu, choose one of these commands:

- **Export to PDF.** An Adobe PDF (Portable Document Format) is useful because it keeps the formatting you select. If you print your report or send it to a relative, the report will look exactly as you see it on your monitor. You can't change a PDF within Family Tree Maker.

- **Export to CSV.** This spreadsheet format organises information into fields (comma-separated values). Although you can export any report to a CSV file, it is most useful for statistical reports that use columns, such as the Marriage report.

- **Export to RTF.** This creates a basic text file but can include information such as font style, size, and colour. This universal format can be read by nearly all text editing applications.

- **Export to HTML.** Hypertext Markup Language is the standard language for creating and formatting Web pages.

3   Select the location where you want to save the report and type a name for it. Then click **Save**.

Printing a Report

When you have finished creating and customising a report, you might want to print it out. Family Tree Maker makes it easy to choose setup options and print a report.

1   Access the report you want to print.

2   Click the **Print** button above the editing panel.

3 When prompted, choose a printer, select the number of copies, and choose a page range.

4 Click **Print**.

Sharing a Report

You can share your reports with others by emailing them in a choice of formats.

Note: You must be connected to the Internet and have a desktop email application to use this feature.

1 Access the report you want to email.

2 Click the **Share** button above the editing panel. From the pop-up menu, choose one of these commands:

- **Send as PDF.** An Adobe PDF retains printer formatting and graphical elements so it resembles how the printed document will appear.

- **Send as CSV.** This format organises information into fields (comma-separated values) and is intended for importing into spreadsheet applications.

- **Send as RTF.** This creates a basic text file but can include information such as font style, size, and colour. This universal format can be read by nearly all text editing applications.

- **Send as Image.** This option lets you create an image of the report as a bitmap, JPEG, and other image formats.

3 Change any options as necessary and click **Save**. Family Tree Maker opens a new email with the file automatically attached in your default email application.

4 Send the email as you would any other.

Chapter Eleven
Creating a Family History Book

Wouldn't you love to have a printed history of your family so you could share your family stories, photographs, maps, and research? And what could be more convenient than using the same software to organise your family history *and* create a book to tell your ancestral story?

Family Tree Maker has a publishing tool to help you create a high quality family history book that you and your family will enjoy for years to come. This is a desktop book-building feature that's built into the Family Tree Maker software. It's a great way to assemble a traditional genealogy using images, facts, charts, and reports from your tree.

The Desktop Book-Building Tool

Getting started with the book-building tool is easy because you can use the facts, charts, reports, and timelines already in your tree. Add some personal stories and photos and you've created a book you can email to family members or get printed at a high street printers.

Starting a Family History Book

1 Go to the **Collection** tab on the Publish workspace. In **Publication Types**, select **Books**.

2 Double-click **Genealogy Book**. The Save Book dialog opens.

3   Type a title for the book in the **Book Name** field and click **Save**. The book opens in the text editor.

Accessing a Saved Book

1   Go to the **Collection** tab on the Publish workspace. In **Publication Types**, select **Saved Books**.

2   Double-click the book you want to open, or select its icon and click the **Detail** tab. The book opens in the text editor.

Setting Up a Book

When you create a book you can enter the name of the author and title and add headers and footers.

1   Access the book you want to set up.

2   In the book outline toolbar, click the **Book Properties** button.

3   Change the book's properties as necessary:

- **Book Title.** Type the name of the book. This is the title that will appear in the book's headers and footers; it is not added to the title page automatically.

- **Author.** Type the author of the book.

- **Header.** Choose a header type from the pop-up menu. Headers are typically the title of a book, but you can have no header, or a combination of the book title, chapter name, and page number. To change the header's font, click **Change Font** and select a style and size.

Note: You can change the header for a specific page using Item Properties. For instructions, see "Changing an Item's Settings" on page 211.

- **Footer.** Choose a footer type from the pop-up menu. Footers are typically page numbers, but you can have no footer, or a combination of the book title, chapter name, and page number. To change the footer's font, click **Change Font** and select a style and size.

   Note: You can add or remove the footer from a specific page using Item Properties. For instructions, see "Changing an Item's Settings" on page 211.

- **Page Numbers Use Roman Numerals.** Select this checkbox to use standard Roman numerals (i, ii, iii, iv) for the book's front matter—title page, table of contents, dedication, etc.

- **Starting number.** Choose what page you want the body of the book to start on (the front matter—title page, table of contents, dedication, etc.—will be numbered separately).

4 Click **OK**.

Adding Content to a Book

You can add any number of items to your family history book, including stories, photos, reports, charts, and even an automatically generated table of contents and index.

Adding Text

Don't let your family history book become a dry recitation of facts. Add interest by including family stories and memories. If your great-uncle emigrated to America when he was young, don't just list this fact in an individual report. Include an excerpt from his diary that tells how he felt when saw the Statue of Liberty.

Family Tree Maker has two options for entering text: you can manually type text or import text from another text file or document.

Adding a Smart Story (Text Item)

Before you can add text, you'll need to add a text item to the book. A text item is basically a blank sheet of paper in the book's text editor. Creating one is much like opening a new document in a word-processing program. You can use it to create everything from an entire chapter to a simple page with a photo and a caption.

1 Access the book you want to add a text item to. In the book outline toolbar, click the **Add Book Item** button.

2 Select **Other**. Then double-click **Smart Story (Text Item)**, or select its icon and click **Add**. A blank page opens.

Entering Text Manually

You can use the text editor to write your own family narratives.

1 Select a text item in the book outline.

2 Place the insertion point where you want the text to be and begin typing.

Importing Text from Another Document

If you've already written part of your book in another text editing application, you don't have to re-type your text or copy and paste sections into Family Tree Maker. You can import the entire .doc/.docx, .rtf/.rtfd, or .txt document at once—without losing formatting.

1 Select a text item in the book outline.

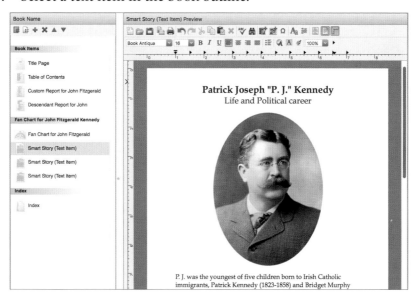

2 Place the insertion point where you want the text to be; then click the Open Document button in the text editor toolbar.

3 Navigate to the document you want to import and click **Open**.

Formatting Text

The text formatting options available in Family Tree Maker are similar to most word processing applications. You can change fonts, text size, and spacing.

1 Select a text item in the book outline.

2 Format the text using these options:

- **Change the font colour, size, or style.** Select the text you want to change. Control-click and choose **Character** from the shortcut menu. The Font dialog opens. Make any necessary changes and close the dialog.

- **Change the amount of space between lines of text.** Select a paragraph. Control-click and choose **Paragraph** from the shortcut menu. Click the arrows next to **Inter-line spacing** to change the spacing. Click **OK**.

- **Change the amount of space between paragraphs.** Select the paragraphs. Control-click and choose **Paragraph** from the shortcut menu. Click the arrows next to **Paragraph spacing** to change the spacing. Click **OK**.

Adding Images

What family history book would be complete without photos, letters, historical records, and maps? Family Tree Maker lets you add images from your family tree or images you've stored on your computer that you don't necessarily want to keep in your family tree—for example, clip art or embellishments.

1 Select a text item in the book outline.

2 Place the insertion point where you want the image to appear.

Note: In the book-building tool you cannot wrap text around images. If you don't want the image to be in-line with the text, you may want to add space before and after the object.

3 Do one of the following:

- To use an image from your tree, click the **Insert image from media collection** button in the text editor toolbar. Select the image and click **OK**.

- To use an image from your computer, click the **Insert image from file** button in the text editor toolbar. Navigate to the image you want and click **Open**.

4 To define how the image interacts with text, Control-click it and choose "In Line," "Top and Bottom," "Square," "Behind Text," or "In Front of Text" from the **Text Wrapping** shortcut menu. You can also move the image by dragging it to a new location.

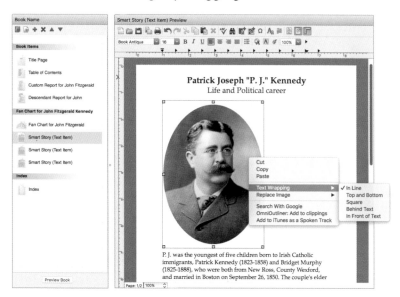

5 To resize an image, select it. Then drag a selection handle to change the size. To maintain the image's proportions, drag the image from a corner.

Adding a Chart or Report

You can add as many charts and reports to a book as you like. Make sure you choose ones that are appropriate for your audience. For example, you may want to share more personal and informal reports in a book meant for your children, but you'll want to remove facts about living relatives if you are sharing the book with other genealogists.

1   Access the book you want to add a chart or report to. In the book outline toolbar, click the **Add Book Item**  button.

2   In the Add Book Item dialog, select the category for the chart or report you want to use. Then double-click the chart/report, or select its icon and click **Add**.

Tip: You can also select **Saved Charts** or **Saved Reports** to use documents you've already created.

3   Use the editing panel to customise the chart or report (for instructions, see chapters 9 and 10).

Adding a Placeholder

If you want to incorporate a story, chart, or photo from outside Family Tree Maker, you can use a placeholder to reserve a specific number of pages until you're ready to add the information.

1   Access the book you want to add a placeholder to. In the book outline toolbar, click the **Add Book Item**  button.

2   In the Add Book Item dialog, select **Other**. Then double-click **Place Holder**, or select its icon and click **Add**.

3   Choose the number of pages you want to reserve using the **Number of pages** arrows.

Tip: Give the placeholder a descriptive name so you don't forget what you were going to use it for. You can change its name by clicking the Book Item Properties button in the book outline toolbar.

Creating a Table of Contents

Family Tree Maker can generate a table of contents for a book automatically. If you make changes to a book (such as adding a chart or moving a chapter), the table of contents and its page numbers will be updated to reflect the changes.

Note: The table of contents is added after the title page. You can change the order of the front matter—table of contents, dedication, preface, etc.—but you cannot move the table of contents out of the front matter.

1   Access the book you want to add a table of contents to. In the book outline toolbar, click the **Add Book Item** ➕ button.

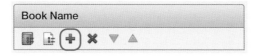

2   In the Add Book Item dialog, select **Other**. Then double-click **Table of Contents**, or select its icon and click **Add**. The table of contents opens.

Although you cannot edit the table of contents, you can customise its font, size, and colour by clicking the Fonts button under the "Table of Contents Options" heading.

Creating an Index of Individuals

Family Tree Maker can automatically generate a list of all individuals in the book's reports and charts (names mentioned in text items will *not* be included). If you make changes to the book (such as adding a new chart) Family Tree Maker will update the index to reflect the change.

Note: The index cannot be moved; it must be the last item in your book.

1   Access the book you want to add an index to. In the book outline toolbar, click the **Add Book Item** ✚ button.

2   In the Add Book Item dialog, select **Other**. Then double-click **Index**, or select its icon and click **Add**. The index opens.

   Although you cannot edit the index, you can customise its font, size, and colour by clicking the Fonts button under the "Index Options" heading.

Organising a Book

As your book grows, you may find that it has changed from the project you originally envisioned and that you need to make some adjustments. Perhaps you've uncovered additional records and photos and you want to rearrange a couple of chapters to include them. Family Tree Maker makes it easy to change titles, move chapters, or even delete sections you don't need.

Changing an Item's Settings

A Family Tree Maker book is made up of a variety of different book items: text items, charts, reports, etc. You can change settings for each book item.

1   Select an item in the book outline.

2   In the book outline toolbar, click the **Book Item Properties**  button.

The Item Properties dialog opens.

3   Change the item's settings using these options:

- **Change the item's title.** Type a title in the **Item Name** field. This is the title that will appear in the book's table of contents and this item's headers and footers.

- **Make this item start a new chapter.** Select the **This item begins a chapter** checkbox.

- **Make the first page of this item start on an odd-numbered (right-facing) page.** Select the **Start this item on an odd numbered page** checkbox. Typically each chapter starts on an odd-numbered page.

- **Prevent a page number from appearing on the first page of an item.** Select the **Do not print page number on the first page** checkbox. Typically chapter openers do not include a page number. You may also want to use this option for reports, charts, and full-page images.

- **Display headers in the item.** Select the **Include the header in this item** checkbox.

- **Display footers in the item.** Select the **Include the footer in this item** checkbox.

4   Click **OK**.

Rearranging Book Items

The book panel shows all the items in a book. The order in which they're displayed in this outline is the order in which they'll be printed. You can change this order at any time.

1   Select an item in the book outline.

2   To change an item's order in the outline, select the item. Then click the **Move Up** ▲ and **Move Down** ▼ arrows in the book outline toolbar. (You can also drag items to the place you want.)

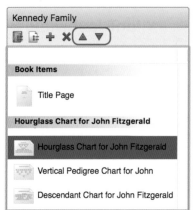

Deleting a Book Item

If you don't want a text item, report, or chart in your book, you can delete it.

1 Select an item in the book outline.

2 Click the **Delete Book Item** ✖ button.

Printing a Book at Home

When you've finished creating your book, you can print out copies on your printer at home.

> Tip: If you want to see what your book will look like when it is printed, click the **Preview Book** button below the book outline.

1 Access the book you want to print.

2 Click the **Print** button below the main toolbar.

3 When prompted choose a printer, select the number of copies, and choose a page range.

4 Click **Print**.

Exporting a Book

You can export your book as a PDF or text file and take it to a good quality high street printers to be printed and professionally bound. You can also email the file to family members.

1 Access the book you want to export; then click the **Share** button below the main toolbar.

2 Choose an export option from the pop-up menu.

3 Change any options as necessary and click **Save**.

Part Four
Managing Your Trees

Chapter 12: Working with Trees 217

Chapter 13: Tools and Preferences 241

Chapter 14: Family Tree Problem Solver 265

Chapter Twelve
Working with Trees

In chapter 3 you learnt how to create and import new trees. This chapter explains how to use the wealth of tools Family Tree Maker has to help you manage, share, and protect your trees.

Managing Your Trees

This section explains how to manage your trees effectively, whether you're working on one all-inclusive tree or several trees.

Opening a Tree

When you launch Family Tree Maker, it automatically opens the last tree you were working on. You can switch to a different tree whenever you need to.

1   On the main toolbar, click the tree shortcut menu and choose the tree you want.

If the tree you want isn't in the list, click **Browse** to look for it on your hard drive. Navigate to the tree you want and click **Open**.

Note: If you try to open a GEDCOM, a tree file from a previous version of Family Tree Maker, or a file from another genealogy program, the software automatically opens the New Tree tab so you can import it (for instructions, see "Importing a Tree File" on page 24).

Viewing Information About a Tree

You can view a summary of your tree file, such as its size and the last time you created a backup of it. You can also see statistics about the people in your tree, for example, the numbers of individuals, marriages, and surnames.

1 Go to the **Current Tree** tab on the Plan workspace. A basic summary of your tree file appears at the top of the workspace.

2 To see additional statistics, click the **More** button. The Statistical Information dialog opens.

Renaming a Tree

1 On the main toolbar, click the tree shortcut menu, move the pointer over the tree name, and then choose **Rename Tree**.

2 Type a name for the tree and click **OK**.

Note: You can change the name of a tree at any time. Only the name of your FTM tree will change. The name of any linked Ancestry trees will not be changed.

Deleting a Tree

1   On the main toolbar, click the tree shortcut menu, move the pointer over the tree name, and then choose **Delete Tree**.

2   If you want to delete the media files that are linked to the tree, select **Move selected attachments** and select the files you'd like to delete. Then click **Move to Trash**.

Using Privacy Mode

If your tree contains personal information about living family members, you might want to "privatise" your tree before exporting a family history book or printing a family tree chart. In privacy mode information about living individuals, such as birth dates, will not be displayed. Bear in mind that you cannot edit the tree again until you turn off privacy mode.

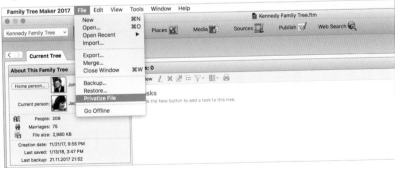

1   Choose **File>Privatize File**. "Privatized" appears in the title bar and a checkmark, or tick, appears next to the **Privatize File** command in the **File** menu.

2   To continue working on your tree, turn off privacy mode by choosing **File>Privatize File** again.

Exporting a Tree File

If you want to share your family tree with someone, you can export all or part of a tree as a GEDCOM, the standard file format used to transfer data between different genealogy software. (Note that images, audio files, and videos cannot be included in GEDCOMs.) You can also export your tree as a Family Tree Maker file; however, it will be compatible only with the version it was created in.

> Tip: To export a particular branch of your family tree, go to the People workspace. Select the person whose family you want to export. Control-click and choose **Export Branch**.

1   Choose **File>Export**. If an information message appears, click **OK**. The Export dialog opens.

2   Do one of the following:

- To export the entire tree, select **Entire file**.

- To select specific individuals to include in the file, select **Selected individuals**. A dialog opens. Select an individual then click **Include** to add the person. When you've finished selecting individuals, click **OK**.

- To export a saved Index list, click **Saved List**.

GEDCOM

If your great-aunt is also compiling a family history but does not use the same software you do, you'll need to share your family tree with her in GEDCOM format. GEDCOM stands for GEnealogical Data COMmunications; it allows genealogy files to be opened in any genealogy software program—on Macs or PCs.

3 Choose a GEDCOM or Family Tree Maker option from the **Output format** pop-up menu.

4 Choose the information you want included in the exported file:

- **Privatize living people.** Select this checkbox to exclude information about living individuals. Names and relationships will be exported but facts and shared facts will not.

- **Private facts.** Select this checkbox to export facts marked as private.

- **Private notes.** Select this checkbox to export notes marked as private.

- **Media files.** Select this checkbox to export all media files in your tree except for media marked as private.

- **Private media.** Select this checkbox to export media files marked as private.

- **Tasks.** Select this checkbox to export your research to-do list. This option is not available for GEDCOMs.

- **Charts, reports, and books.** Select this checkbox to export charts, reports, and books you've saved. This option is not available for GEDCOMs.

- **Include only items linked to selected individuals.** Click this checkbox to export only tasks, notes, and media items that are linked to the individuals you're exporting.

5 Depending on the output format you have chosen, select the **Enable password protection** checkbox or the **Export as password-protected ZIP file** checkbox. The **Password** and **Confirm password** fields become available. Enter the password you want to use for protection of your exported tree. Make sure your password is not easy to guess. It should be **at least eight characters long** and contain digits as well as letters. You, or anyone you give the file to, will have to enter exactly the same password when opening or unpacking your exported tree. Passwords cannot be recovered, so it's a good idea to write the password down and keep it in a safe place.

6 Click **Export**.

7 Navigate to the location where you want to save the tree file.

> Note: Family Tree Maker automatically gives the exported tree file the same name as the original tree. If you want to use a different name, you can change it.

8 Click **Save**. A message tells you when your tree file has been exported successfully.

Backing Up Tree Files

Your family trees are important; not only do they contain your family's history, they represent hours of hard work. Unfortunately, computer files can be corrupted by viruses or accidentally deleted. You can preserve your family history through regular backups. Then, if your original tree is damaged or you want to revert to a previous copy, you can restore it from the backup.

> Tip: Family Tree Maker can back up your tree automatically every time you close the application. If you want this happen, choose **Family Tree Maker 2017>Preferences** and select the **Back up tree file automatically** checkbox.

Backing Up a Tree File

1   Make sure the tree you want to back up is open and choose
    File>Backup. The **Backup the Tree** dialog opens.

2   If you want a new name to distinguish your backup file from
    your original tree, type a new name in the **Backup Filename**
    field. For example, if you back up your trees to the same USB
    flash drive every time, and this backup file has the same name
    as the tree file that is already on the drive, then this backup
    will write over the original file.

3   Select the **Media files** checkbox to back up media files in the
    tree's media folder.

4   Select the **Historical events** checkbox to back up historical
    events referred to in the tree.

5   Select the **Web favorites** checkbox to include your favourites list
    from the Web Search workspace.

6 If the tree is linked to an Ancestry tree, select the **Allow restored file to resume syncing** checkbox so the backup file can be synced with the Ancestry tree if necessary.

7 Select one of these backup types:

- **DVD or flash drive.** Select **Removable media**. In the pop-up menu, choose your DVD drive or flash drive.

- **Hard disk.** Select **Default location of trees** to save the backup to the folder where your current tree is saved; select **Custom directory** to select a new location on your hard disk.

8 Click **Backup**. A message tells you when the tree file has been backed up successfully.

Note: Backup files cannot be opened in other genealogy applications like GEDCOMs can. They can only be opened with the version of Family Tree Maker in which they were created.

Restoring a Tree from a Backup

If you need to use your backup file as your working tree, you can restore it when necessary.

1 If your backup file has been copied to a removable media, copy it back to your hard disk.

2 Choose **File>Restore**. A file management dialog opens.

3 Navigate to the backup file you want to restore and click **Open**.

Note: You can identify a backup file by its file extension (the letters after the file name). Family Tree Maker for Mac backups use .ftmb.

The tree will open. Any information you have entered in the original tree since you created this backup will not be included.

Compressing a Tree File

As you work on a tree you will add and delete quite a bit of information. However, even when you delete information, the tree file size may not change. You should compress your tree every so often to remove unnecessary bits of data and optimise performance.

1   Choose **Tools**>**Compact File**.

2   To back up your tree file before you compress it, select the **Back up file before compacting** checkbox (recommended).

3   To have the tree file analysed more deeply prior to compacting, select the **Perform extended analysis** option. This may significantly increase the duration of the compacting process.

4   Click **Compact**. If you chose to back up your tree file, the Backup dialog opens. Change any options and click **Backup**.

5   When Family Tree Maker has finished compacting the tree file, a message appears showing how much the file size was reduced by. Click **OK**.

6   Repeat steps 1 through 5 until you get the result "reduced by 0.00%" or as close as you can get to it.

Because file compression happens behind the scenes, you won't see any changes in your tree, but you should notice better performance and a smaller overall tree file size.

Uploading a Tree to Ancestry

Chapter 3 explains how to start a new tree by downloading an existing tree from Ancestry. Family Tree Maker also lets you upload a tree to Ancestry. It's easy, free, and because your tree will be online, it can be shared with family around the world.

Note: To upload a tree to Ancestry, you do not need a subscription, but you must have an Ancestry account and Internet access.

Uploading and Linking a Tree to Ancestry

When you upload a tree to Ancestry, you create a link between your desktop Family Tree Maker tree and its corresponding tree on Ancestry. This means that additions, deletions, or edits you make in your Family Tree Maker tree will be duplicated in your Ancestry tree (and vice versa). (For more information, see "Working with Linked Trees" on page 229.)

Please be aware that the time it takes to upload your tree is determined by the tree size (including the size of the media collection) and the speed of your Internet connection. Your tree will be transmitted in the background in two stages. Media items are processed first and data is uploaded during the final stage. The tree will appear online when both the media and tree data have been uploaded.

Note: When you upload and link a tree to Ancestry, you must upload your entire tree; you can't choose which people in your tree are uploaded.

1   Open the tree you want to upload to Ancestry. Then go to the Plan workspace and click the **Current Tree** tab.
2   Click the **Upload and Link to Ancestry** button.
3   Enter a name in the **Ancestry tree name** field.
4   Choose whether you want to make your Ancestry tree public or private. See "Privacy Options for Ancestry Trees" below for more information.
5   If you don't want your private tree to appear in search results on Ancestry or third-party search engines such as Google, select the **Exclude this tree from Ancestry search index** checkbox.
6   Choose whether your Ancestry and FTM trees will be synced manually or automatically. (For more information on syncing options, see "Setting Up Syncing" on page 230.)

7 Click **Upload**. A message lets you know when the tree has been uploaded successfully.

8 To view your tree on Ancestry, select the **View online tree now** checkbox and click **OK**.

Privacy Options for Ancestry Trees

When you upload your tree to Ancestry, you can choose between two levels of privacy:

- **Public.** If your tree is public, Ancestry subscribers can view your entire tree (apart from information about living individuals and private notes), and your tree will appear on search engines such as Google.

- **Private.** If your tree is private, limited information about individuals in your tree (name, birth year, birthplace) will still appear in Ancestry search results. No one will be able to view your entire tree or any attached photos and records unless he or she asks your permission and you grant it. You can also invite other people to view your tree.

Differences Between FTM and Ancestry Trees

Most content in your tree is uploaded and/or synced seamlessly between Family Tree Maker and Ancestry. However, because Ancestry and Family Tree Maker trees are in different formats, there are a few differences you should be aware of.

Content	Differences
Facts	In general, fact dates, names, places, and descriptions (including alternate facts) are the same in Family Tree Maker and Ancestry trees. However, some fact types have different labels. For example, the Physical Description fact in Family Tree Maker is the Description fact in Ancestry trees.
Notes	In Family Tree Maker you can create a variety of notes: person, research, fact, relationship, media, and source citation. Only person notes can be uploaded to Ancestry trees.
Media items	• The caption of a media item in Family Tree Maker is the same as the **Picture name** field on Ancestry. • Video items are not transferred between Family Tree Maker and Ancestry. • Media items attached to relationships in Family Tree Maker are uploaded to Ancestry as linked to each person individually, but not to the relationship. • Ancestry citation media you've merged into Family Tree Maker won't be re-uploaded to Ancestry. • Documents in these formats can't be uploaded to Ancestry tree: .exe, .dll, .bat, .htm/.html, and .mht. • Photos that exceed 15MB will be resized when uploaded to Ancestry—your original file will not be affected. Images need to be in one of these formats: .jpeg, .bmp, .png, .gif, or .tiff.

Content	Differences
Places	Shortened place names and GPS coordinates in Family Tree Maker are not uploaded to Ancestry trees.
Publications	Saved reports, charts, and books cannot be transferred from Family Tree Maker to Ancestry.
Privacy	In Family Tree Maker only you can view information you've entered for a living individual. In your Ancestry tree, only people you give permission to can view information about living individuals.
Sources	• Sources created with templates will transfer to Ancestry. Some fields cannot be uploaded online. • Media items attached to citations are uploaded; media items attached to sources are not.
Stories	A story created on Ancestry will become a .htm file in Family Tree Maker, which can be viewed in a Web browser. You can edit the text in a word-processing program.
Web links	Web links are not uploaded, downloaded, or synced.

Working with Linked Trees

Family Tree Maker makes entering information into your tree quick and easy. It also contains powerful tools to help you organise your media items, cite sources, and create charts and reports. But because the program is on your desktop, sharing your tree with others can be time-consuming, and, if you don't have a laptop, you won't have access to your tree when you're away from home.

Fortunately, FamilySync gives you the freedom to view and update your tree no matter where you are. First, create your tree in Family Tree Maker. Then upload and link it to Ancestry. When you go to the library or to stay with a relative—anywhere with Internet access—make changes to your tree online. Then sync the changes to your FTM tree when you get home. (You can also download and link a tree you've already created on Ancestry. For more information, see "Downloading a Tree from Ancestry" on page 26.)

Each Ancestry tree can link to multiple FTM trees. It's not necessary to break an old link to download a tree to a new computer. To link the trees on multiple computers to a single Ancestry tree, follow these steps:

1   Back up your FTM tree manually, including media and sync information. (See "Backing Up a Tree File", page 223).

2   Copy the backup file to another computer using a USB flash drive.

3   On the other computer, restore your tree from the backup.

The changes made in any of the trees can be applied to other trees automatically or manually. The core data in your linked trees is synchronised in all directions. But some types of data will not sync, remaining only on the computer they were created on.

Note: For more information on what does and doesn't sync, open Family Tree Maker Help from the **Help** menu and search for the "Syncing Local and Online Trees" topic.

Setting Up Syncing

When you link your FTM and Ancestry trees together, you can choose how your trees will be synced. You have two options:

- **Manually.** You can sync your trees by clicking the **Sync Now** button on the **Current Tree** tab or clicking the Ancestry Sync icon and choosing "Sync Now" from the pop-up menu.

- **Automatically.** Family Tree Maker checks for changes when you open a tree or close the program. If it detects differences between the trees, it syncs the changes automatically. You can also sync your trees anytime by clicking the Sync Now button on the Current Tree tab.

You can also choose whether or not Family Tree Maker will display a list of changes you've made to your Ancestry and FTM trees for you to review before syncing.

Changing Your Current Sync Setting

When you upload or download a linked tree, you will choose how your trees will be synced. You can change this setting at any time.

1   Go to the **Current Tree** tab on the Plan workspace.

2   Click the **Sync Now** button and choose "Sync Options" from the pop-up menu. The Sync Options dialog opens.

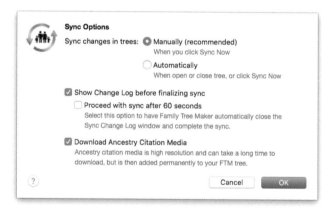

3   Select **Automatically** or **Manually**. Then click **OK**.

Creating a Log of Recent Sync Activity

You can set up FamilySync so that every time you sync your Ancestry and FTM trees you can view a list of changes—the number of people, sources, and media items that have been added, updated, or deleted from your tree since the last sync.

1   Go to the **Current Tree** tab on the Plan workspace.

2   Click the **Sync Now** button and choose "Sync Options" from the pop-up menu. The Sync Options dialog opens.

3   Select the **Show Change Log before finalizing sync** checkbox.

4   Select the **Proceed with sync after 60 seconds** checkbox if you want Family Tree Maker to automatically close the Sync Change Log window and complete the sync.

5   Click **OK**. The next time your trees are synced, you'll see the Sync Change Log (fig. 12-1).

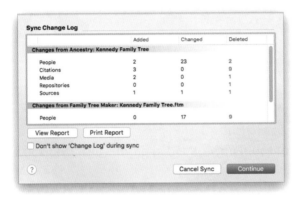

Figure 12-1. The Sync Change Log.

To proceed with the sync, click the **Continue** button. To reject the changes, click the **Cancel Sync** button. Click the **View Report** button to see specific details about what changes will be included in the sync.

Viewing a Tree's Sync Status

The Ancestry Sync icon in the upper-right corner lets you see at a glance whether your FTM and Ancestry tree are synced. A check mark icon means that the trees are up-to-date; an icon with two vertical arrows means that changes waiting to be synced (fig. 12-2).

The Ancestry Sync icon also displays the sync weather report status. See "Getting Sync Weather Reports" below for more information.

Figure 12-2. Left, trees are in sync; right, trees need to be synced.

You can also see the date and time when your tree was last synced on the Current Tree tab on the Plan workspace (fig. 12-3).

Figure 12-3. Date and time of last sync.

Syncing Trees Manually

You can sync your tree manually anytime. However, bear in mind that you can't work with your Ancestry or FTM tree until syncing is complete. This may take from a few seconds to a few minutes.

On the Plan workspace, click the **Current Tree** tab; then click the **Sync Now** button. On other workspaces, click the Ancestry Sync icon and choose "Sync Now" from the pop-up menu.

> Note: You can't sync your trees from Ancestry; you must use Family Tree Maker. To see the changes in your Ancestry tree, you'll need to reload the Ancestry website in your browser.

Getting Sync Weather Reports

Wouldn't it be great if you could know when there was a problem with syncing so you could just stay away for a while and come back when it was safe? Now every time you go to sync, if there's a reason why you may want to think twice, a window pops up to say so. The red window appears if the sync system is down, or if syncing is downright dangerous for some reason. This status is actually a kind of "kill switch", and syncing is temporarily disabled. The orange window appears when caution is in order. You can still sync but the Weather Report message system lets us tell you what conditions are like.

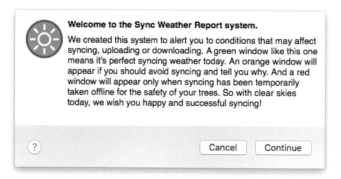

In fact, you don't even have to try syncing a tree to find out what the sync weather is like. Just take a look at the Ancestry Sync icon, which can be found in the top-right corner of the application window and in the FamilySync panel in the bottom-left part of the Current Tree tab on the Plan workspace. It not only displays the sync status, it lets you instantly see the latest weather report as well:

 No problems found, safe to sync.

 Problems may occur, syncing is not recommended.

 Serious connection problems, syncing is impossible.

Resolving Conflicts Between Linked Trees

When you change the same fact in your FTM and Ancestry trees, you'll need to choose which information to keep (fig. 12-4). For example, if you change a birthplace in Family Tree Maker and a family member changes the same birthplace in your Ancestry tree, when you try to sync your trees, you'll be prompted to fix the issue.

1   Do one of the following:

•   To keep the information entered in Family Tree Maker, select **Overwrite conflicts with Family Tree Maker data**.

•   To keep the information entered in the Ancestry tree, select **Overwrite conflicts with Ancestry data**.

•   To manually choose which information to keep, select **Resolve conflicts manually**.

Figure 12-4. A message showing conflicts between linked trees.

2   Click **Next**. If you are overwriting data, the sync continues. If you are resolving the conflict manually, choose the facts you want to keep and click **Continue**.

Important: Deletions always take priority over other changes. For example, if you delete an individual in your Ancestry tree and change the same individual's birthplace in your FTM tree, when you sync the trees together the individual will be deleted.

Unlinking Trees

If you no longer want your FTM and Ancestry trees linked together, you can sever the connection between them.

> Warning: If you unlink your FTM and Ancestry trees, changes will no longer be synced, and you cannot relink the trees, but you can upload or download the tree again to create a new link. Also note that Ancestry hints will not appear in an unlinked tree.

1   Go to the **Current Tree** tab on the Plan workspace.

2   Click the **Sync Now** button and choose "Unlink Tree" from the pop-up menu.

Changing Privacy Settings

When you upload a tree to Ancestry, you choose whether your online tree will be public (the default option) or private. However, you can change its privacy settings at any time. (For more information on the differences between public and private trees, see page 227.)

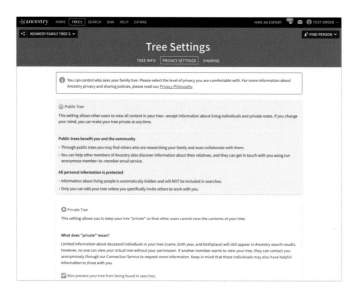

1   Go to the **Current Tree** tab on the Plan workspace.

2   Click the **Sync Now** button and choose "Manage Online Tree Privacy" from the pop-up menu. The Tree Settings page opens.

3   Select **Public Tree** to let Ancestry subscribers view your tree; select **Private Tree** to prevent others from viewing your tree.

> Note: If your tree is private, Ancestry subscribers can still see names, birth dates, and birthplaces in search results. However, to see your full tree or any attached photos and records, they'll have to ask you for permission. If you don't want your tree to appear in search results, select the **Also prevent your tree from being found in searches** checkbox.

4   Click Save Changes.

Inviting Others to View Your Tree

You can invite friends and family to view your Ancestry tree. You can even let them add new information or photos.

1   Go to the **Current Tree** tab on the Plan workspace.

2   Click the **Invite to Online Tree** button. The Tree Settings page opens. Click the **Invite people** button.

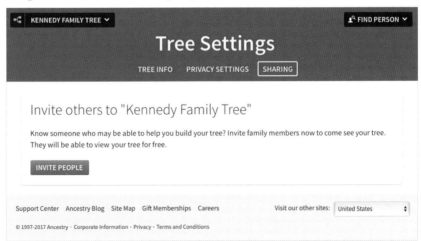

Note: If you've already invited people to your tree, you'll need to click the **Sync Now** button and choose "Manage Online Tree Invitees" to invite more people to your tree.

3 Enter the person's email address or Ancestry username to address the invitation and assign the person one of these roles: editor, contributor, or guest.

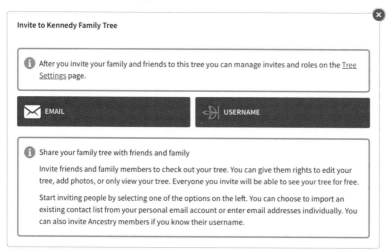

4 If you want, include a personal message to the invitee. Then click **Send Invites**.

Roles in Ancestry Trees

When you invite people to view your tree, they can participate in different ways, depending on the role you assign them:

- **Editor.** Editors can add, edit, or delete anyone in your tree, add stories and photos, and leave comments. They can also see living individuals. Editors cannot delete or rename the tree, change tree settings, or invite others to the tree.

- **Contributor.** Contributors can add photos or stories to your tree, but they cannot add or edit people. You can choose whether or not they see living individuals.

- **Guest.** Guests can only view your tree and leave comments. You can choose whether or not they see living individuals.

Chapter Thirteen
Tools and Preferences

Using Family Tree Maker Tools

If you need some extra assistance in calculating approximate birth dates, understanding how individuals are related to each other, or creating a to-do list, Family Tree Maker has several tools that can help.

Soundex Calculator

Soundex is a term familiar to serious family historians. It's a coding system used by the U.S. government to create indexes of American census records (and passenger lists) based on how a surname sounds rather than how it is spelt. This was done to compensate for potential spelling and transcription errors. For example, "Smith" may be spelt "Smythe", "Smithe", or "Smyth". Using Soundex, these "Smiths" are all identified by the same code (S530). You can use Soundex to find surnames that use the same code and then search for ancestors using all these surname variations.

Choose **Tools>Soundex Calculator**. Type a surname in the **Name** field, or click **Index** to select someone in your tree.

Relationship Calculator

The relationship calculator helps you identify how two people in your tree are related, shows an individual's nearest common relative, and gives his or her canon and civil numbers.

Note: Canon and civil numbers indicate the degree of relationship between individuals. Canon laws (used in the United States) measure the number of steps back to a common ancestor. Civil degree measures the total number of steps from one family member to another.

1   Choose **Tools>Relationship Calculator**. In the first field you'll see the home person. In the second field you'll see the individual who is the current focus of the tree.

2   To change the individuals whose relationship you're calculating, click the **Person from people index** button (the index card) next to a name. In Index of Individuals select a new person and click **OK**.

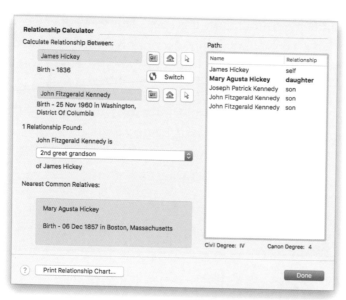

The individuals' relationship is shown underneath their names. If they have multiple connections (for example if they are cousins who married), use the pop-up menu to see each relationship. You can also see how the individuals are related in the Path section.

Date Calculator

You can use the date calculator to work out an individual's year of birth, age at the time of a specific event, or the date of an event. For example, if you know the date on which your grandmother was married and you know how old she was when she got married, you can determine the approximate year she was born in.

1   Choose **Tools>Date Calculator**. The date calculator opens.

2   Use this chart to help you enter dates into the calculator:

To calculate this	Do this
A birth date	• Click **Birth Date**. • Enter a date in the **Date of Known Event** field. • Enter the individual's age in the **Age at Time of Event** fields.
The date of a specific event	• Click **Other Event Date**. • Enter a date in the **Birth Date** field. • Enter the individual's age in the **Age at Time of Event** fields.
An individual's age on a specific date	• Click **Age**. • Enter a date in the **Birth Date** field. • Enter a date in the **Date of Known Event** field.

3   Click **Calculate**. The calculated event date or age appears.

Name Converter

If you import another person's genealogy file into your tree, you may find that each file has recorded names differently; your surnames may be in all caps while theirs may not. You can use the convert names tool to format all names in your tree at once.

1   Choose **Tools>Convert Names**. The Convert Names dialog opens.

2   To capitalise the first letter of each name, select **First Middle Surname**. To capitalise the first letter of the first and middle names and capitalise the entire surname, select **First Middle SURNAME**.

3   Click **Convert**.

Find Individual Tool

You can use any fact in your tree (such as occupation or burial) to locate either a specific individual or a group of individuals who fit specific criteria. For example, you can search for everyone in your tree who lived in Lancashire at the time of the 1851 census. Or, you can find out which individuals are buried in the same cemetery.

Note: The Find Individual tool searches Place and Description fields; Date fields cannot be searched.

1   Choose **Edit>Find Individual**. The Find Individual dialog opens.

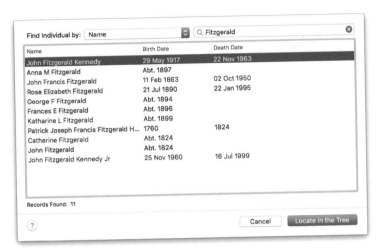

2   Choose the type of fact you want to search from the pop-up menu. Then type a search term and click the search icon (magnifying glass).

3   To view a specific individual, select him or her in the search results and click **Locate in the Tree**.

Automatic Reference Numbers

Some family historians use reference numbers to identify people in their trees, particularly if the tree contains individuals with identical names. Family Tree Maker can assign reference numbers to individuals (Person ID), relationships (Relationship ID), or both.

Note: If you have entered your own reference numbers, Family Tree Maker will not overwrite them.

1   Choose **Tools>References**. The References dialog opens.

2   Select **Individual** to choose how numbers are assigned to individuals; select **Relationship** to choose how numbers are assigned to relationships.

3 Select **Numbers only** to assign numbers, starting with 1. Select **Prefix** to add a prefix before the number (you can enter numbers, letters, and/or symbols). Select **Numbers plus suffix** to add a suffix after the number (you can enter numbers, letters, and/or symbols).

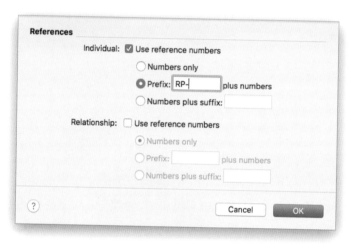

4 Click **OK**.

Global Birth Order Tool

In the family group view, you can change the order in which children are displayed in a family by clicking the Move up and Move down buttons. If you want to have all children in your tree display in birth order, you can use this tool to change them all at once.

1 Choose **Tools>Sort All Children by Birth**.

2 If you want to back up your tree file before you sort children, select the **Back up file before sorting** checkbox (recommended).

3 Click **Sort**.

Research To-Do List

Whether you're a new user or an experienced family historian, the to-do list can help you keep track of the research you've already done and create tasks for your next steps. You can add research tasks for specific individuals or general tasks for your entire tree; tasks can be as simple as sending an email to a cousin or as complicated as locating an entire family in the 1901 UK census.

Creating a To-Do Task

When you create a task, you can choose the priority of the task, the category it fits into, and the date you want to have it completed by (its due date).

> Note: This section explains how to add tasks for specific individuals. You can also add tasks to the tree's to-do list on the Current Tree tab on the Plan workspace.

1   Go to the **Person** tab for a specific individual (on the People workspace). Click the **Tasks** tab.

2   Click the **New** button in the Tasks toolbar. The Task dialog opens.

3   Type a task in the **Description** field. For example, type "Look for Madeline's birth information in Wexford, Ireland".

4 Click **Edit** to enter a category for the task. Select an existing category or create a new one and then click **OK**. (For more information, see "Creating Task Categories" below.)

5 Choose a deadline for the task using the **Due Date** arrows. Then select a priority. (Assign a high priority to the tasks you want to accomplish first.) When you've finished, click **OK**.

Tip: You can print the to-do list for this individual by clicking the Print button in the Tasks toolbar. To print a list of all tasks in your tree, use the Task List Report on the Publish workspace.

Creating Task Categories

Each task you create can be assigned to a category. You can add categories that are useful to your research..

1 Go to the **Current Tree** tab on the Plan workspace. In the Tasks section, you can see your current to-do list.

2 Click **New**. The Task dialog opens. Click **Edit**. The categories dialog opens, showing all available categories.

3   Click the **Add** (+) button.

4   Type a name in the **New Category** field and click **OK**. Click **OK** again.

Marking a Task as Complete

When you finish a task on your to-do list, you'll want to mark it as complete. Go to the **Current Tree** tab on the Plan workspace. In the Tasks section, select the checkbox next to the task.

> Tip: To delete a task, select the task and click the **Delete task** (X) button in the Tasks toolbar.

Sorting the To-Do List

You can filter the to-do list in various ways. For example, you can sort the list to show which tasks have been done or are still pending.

1   Go to the **Current Tree** tab on the Plan workspace.

2   Click the **Filter tasks** button and choose one of these commands from the pop-up menu:

- To show every task you've entered, choose **Show All Tasks**.

- To show unfinished tasks, choose **Show Uncompleted Tasks**.

- To show tasks that belong to a specific category, choose **Filter by Task Categories**.

Tip: You can change what information is displayed for each task. Click the **Show/Hide columns** button in the Tasks toolbar. Then, from the pop-up menu, select or deselect specific columns.

Setting Up Preferences

Family Tree Maker is a powerful program with many features and options. To get the most out of the software, you might want to take a minute or two to define a few key preferences.

General Preferences

You can set some preferences that affect the interface and general workings of Family Tree Maker.

1   Choose **Family Tree Maker 2017>Preferences**, and then click **General**.

2   Change these preferences as necessary:

- **Default Location for New Tree File.** To change the default location where trees are saved on your hard disk, choose **Other** from the pop-up menu and choose a new folder.

- **Back Up Tree File Automatically.** Select this checkbox to create backups of your trees automatically when you quit the application. If your original tree is ever lost or damaged, you can use the backup to restore your information.

- **LDS Information Show.** Select this checkbox if you want to display LDS facts such as sealings and baptisms. This will also add two LDS-specific Person reports to the Publish workspace.

- **When Entering Place Name Check Place Authority.** Select this checkbox if you want Family Tree Maker to compare each place you enter against its database of locations. This option helps you keep your locations in standard formats and consistent throughout your tree.

- **Portrait Crop to Make Picture Fit the Frame.** Select this checkbox to resize portrait images so that they fill the frame.

  Note: The actual images in your tree will not be modified. Also, you cannot choose to resize individual thumbnails. This option resizes every portrait in your tree.

- **Display Media with Caption Instead of Filename.** Select this checkbox to sort media items by the captions you've given them; otherwise, media items will be sorted and displayed by file name.

- **Sync Weather Status: Show on Ancestry Sync Icon.** Select this checkbox to display the sync weather status badge on the Ancestry Sync icon.

- **Merging Default.** Choose a default method of dealing with differences when merging trees. The options are to delete them or to keep as alternatives.

Online Searching Preferences

You can decide whether or not Family Tree Maker should search FamilySearch and Ancestry for matching records and trees when you're connected to the Internet.

1   Choose **Family Tree Maker 2017>Preferences**, and then click **General**.

2   Change these preferences as necessary:

- **Show hints from Ancestry.** Select this checkbox if you want Family Tree Maker to search Ancestry for individuals in your tree when an Internet connection is available.

  You'll see a green leaf (or hint) next to an individual when possible matches have been found. If you deselect this option, you can still search Ancestry for your family members on the Web Search workspace.

- **Exclude Ancestry tree hints.** Select this checkbox to exclude hints from family trees submitted by other Ancestry users.

- **Show hints from FamilySearch.** Select this checkbox if you want Family Tree Maker to search FamilySearch.org for individuals in your tree when an Internet connection is available.

  You'll see a blue square (or hint) next to an individual when possible matches have been found. If you deselect this option, you can still search FamilySearch for your family members on the Web Search workspace.

- **Show Web Search introduction screen.** Select this checkbox to display Web Search help when you begin an online search.

Fastfields

Fastfields save you time by automatically filling in some types of information. Perhaps you noticed as you typed an individual's name that the last name was completed for you. This is because name fields, among others, are Fastfields.

Location Fastfields remember the places you've entered in a tree. As you type a location, Family Tree Maker suggests possible matches. Use the keyboard arrows, mouse or trackpad to highlight the correct location and press **Return** to select it. You can also keep typing a name to override the Fastfields suggestion.

Fastfields Preferences

Fastfields speed up data entry by automatically filling in repetitive data as you type. For example, if you type "Sydney, New South Wales, Australia" in a place field and then go to another place field and begin to type "Syd", Family Tree Maker will recognise the similarity and suggest "Sydney, New South Wales, Australia". By default, all Fastfields are turned on, but you can turn off any you wish.

1   Choose **Family Tree Maker 2017>Preferences**. Click **General**.

2   To turn off Fastfields for a specific field type, deselect the corresponding **Use Fastfields for** checkbox.

Fact Display Preferences

The person editing panel on the Person tab includes a Sources tab. If you want, you can also display media and notes tabs.

1   Choose **Family Tree Maker 2017>Preferences**. Click **General**.

2   Select the **Display Data Linked to Fact** checkbox for each type of tab you want to display on the person editing panel.

Name Preferences

Family Tree Maker lets you determine how names are displayed in the Index on the People workspace. You can include titles, alternative names, and married names for females.

1   Choose **Family Tree Maker 2017>Preferences**, and then click **Dates/Names/Places**.

2   Change these preferences as necessary:

- **Use AKA if available after middle name.** Select this checkbox to have Also Known As names included with the preferred name (for example, Bobbit, Mary Eliza "Mollie").

- **Use AKA if available as an additional entry.** Select this checkbox to give Also Known As names their own entries in the Index (for example, Hannah Willis and Anna Willis).

- **Use titles if available.** Select this checkbox to have titles included with the preferred name (for example, Hoyt, Captain Samuel).

- **Use married name for females.** Select this checkbox to list women by their married (and maiden) names (for example, Hoyt, Maria Hitchcock).

3   If most events recorded in your tree occur in the same country (for example, if most of your ancestors were born and died in England), you may not want to include that country's name in place fields and charts and reports. To keep a country's name from appearing, choose it from the **Home Country** pop-up menu.

Date Preferences

Family Tree Maker lets you change how dates are formatted.

1 Choose **Family Tree Maker 2017>Preferences**, and then click
Dates/Names/Places.

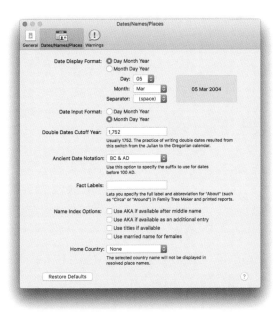

2 Change these date preferences as necessary:

- **Date Display Format.** Choose how dates are displayed. Select
  Day Month Year if you want to show the day before the
  month (10 September 2017). By default, Family Tree Maker
  displays dates in this accepted genealogical date standard.
  Select **Month Day Year** if you want to show the month before
  the day (September 10, 2017).

  Use the pop-up menus to choose different formats for displaying the day, the month, and the date separator.

- **Date Input Format.** Choose how Family Tree Maker interprets dates you type: day, month, year, or month, day, year. For example, if you type "6/7/2010" Family Tree Maker can read this as 6th July 2010 or 7th June 2010.

- **Double Dates Cutoff Year.** Change the year in this field to change the default double date cutoff year. If you do not want double dates to print, set the double date cutoff year to zero.

  Note: Calendars used in Great Britain and its colonies changed in 1752—moving from the Julian to the Gregorian. In the Julian system, the first day of the year was 25 March. In today's Gregorian system, 1 January is the first day of the year. Dates that fall between January and March of 1752 can be interpreted in two ways, and some genealogists prefer to show both dates. For example, 22 February could fall in the year 1750 according to the Gregorian calendar, so the date would be noted as 22 February 1750/51.

- **Ancient Date Notation.** Choose whether dates before 100 AD are displayed as BC/AD or BCE/CE.

- **Fact Labels.** To display a different abbreviation for the term "About" (meaning "circa"), type your preferred label.

Warning and Alert Preferences

Family Tree Maker can automatically check your tree for problems and let you know if it detects a possible error, such as unusual dates.

1   Choose **Family Tree Maker 2017>Preferences**; then click **Warnings**.

2   Change these warning preferences as necessary:

- **Show for unlikely birth, death, and marriage dates.** Select this checkbox to get alerts when you enter dates that aren't accurate (for example, a death date that occurs earlier than a birth date).

- **Show information alerts.** Select this checkbox to get alerts when you update your tree (for example, when you change the home person or edit an individual's name).

- **Show for unrecognized place name.** Select this checkbox to get alerts when Family Tree Maker doesn't recognise a location you've entered.

  Note: This option is not available if you've deselected the "Check Place Authority" checkbox on the General tab.

- **Show when sorting children in the family view.** Select this checkbox to get alerts when you manually sort children in the family group view.

- **Show backup reminder before critical operations.** Select this checkbox to be reminded to back up your tree before performing an operation which may result in data loss.

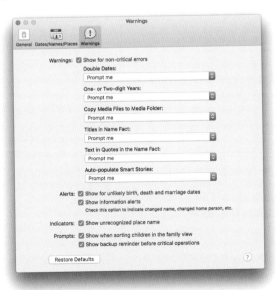

3 Determine how Family Tree Maker handles minor errors:

- **Double Dates.** If Family Tree Maker detects double dates, you can leave the dates as they are, use formatting to show both dates, or be asked what you want to do.

- **One- or Two-Digit Years.** If Family Tree Maker detects years entered with one or two digits, you can leave the date as it is, change the date to the most recent century, or be asked what you want to do.

- **Copy Media Files to Media Folder.** You can choose whether or not media files you add to your tree are automatically copied the file to the Family Tree Maker media folder, or if you are asked what you want to do each time.

- **Titles in Name Fact.** If Family Tree Maker detects a title such as Reverend, Captain, or Sir in a Name fact, you can leave the title in the Name fact, move the title to the Title fact, or be asked what you want to do.

- **Text in Quotes in the Name Fact.** If Family Tree Maker detects nicknames (indicated by quotation marks) in a Name fact, you can leave the nickname in the Name fact, move the nickname to the AKA fact, or be asked what you want to do.

Managing Facts

Facts are the essential building blocks of your tree, where you record the details about your family. In order to better conserve the information you feel is important, you might want to create your own facts or change which fields appear in predefined facts.

Creating a Custom Fact

You can create custom facts that work for your family tree. For example, if you are tracking your ancestors through census records, you can make a custom fact for each census year.

1   Choose **Edit>Manage Facts**. The Manage Facts dialog opens.

2   Click the **Add (+)** button. The Add Custom Fact dialog opens.

3   Change the fact as necessary:

- **Fact label.** Type the name of the fact as it will appear on the Person tab.

- **Short label.** Type a short name (up to six characters) for the fact that will appear on the Tree tab editing panel.

- **Abbreviation.** Type an abbreviation (up to three characters) for the fact that will appear in reports.

- **Fact Type.** Select **Individual fact** if the fact applies to one person, such as birth or death. Select **Shared fact** if the fact applies to more than one individual, such as marriage.

- **Fact Elements.** Select the fields that you want to appear for the fact: Date and Place; Date, Place, and Description; or Description only.

4   Click **Add Fact**.

Modifying a Predefined Fact

While you can't rename or delete predefined facts, you can choose which fields are included as part of the fact. For example, you can modify the Cause of Death fact so that only the Description field is included.

1   Choose **Edit>Manage Facts**. The Manage Facts dialog opens.

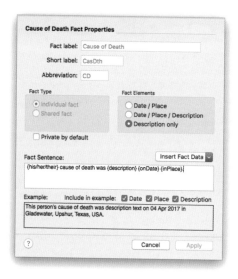

2   Select the predefined fact that you want to modify. Then click **Properties**. The Fact Properties dialog opens.

3   In **Fact Elements**, select which fields you want for the fact. Then click **Apply**.

Modifying a Fact Sentence

When you create an Ahnentafel or descendant report, Family Tree Maker generates descriptive sentences for each fact or event. You can change the wording of these sentences and choose what information is included. For example, the default burial sentence looks like this: Robert Gedge was buried on 1 Sept 1888 in Attleborough, England. If you record cemetery names, you could add this to the sentence: Robert Gedge was buried in All Saints Cemetery in Attleborough, England, on 1 Sept 1888.

1   Choose **Edit>Manage Facts**. The Manage Facts dialog opens.

2   Click the **Add (+)** button or select the fact you want to modify and click **Properties**. The Fact Properties dialog opens. The Fact sentence field shows the current sentence—a combination of text and predefined data variables.

3   To change the text, just add, delete, or type over it. To change which variables are in the sentence, delete the variable or choose a new one from the **Insert Fact Data** pop-up menu.

Tip: If you don't like your changes and want to go back to using the default sentence, click **Insert Fact Data** and choose **Reset Fact Sentence**.

The Example field shows what the fact sentence will look like. For example, if you deselect the Description checkbox, you can see what the sentence will be if the Description field for the fact is blank.

Managing Historical Events

An individual's timeline and the Timeline report can include historical events. You can edit or delete any historical event. You can also add entries that are relevant to your family history, such as international events that caused your ancestors to emigrate.

1   Click **Edit>Manage Historical Events**. The Manage Historical Events window opens.

2   To delete an event, click the entry; then click **Delete**.

3 To add an event, click the **New** button. The Add/Edit Historical Event window opens.

4 Change the historical event as necessary:

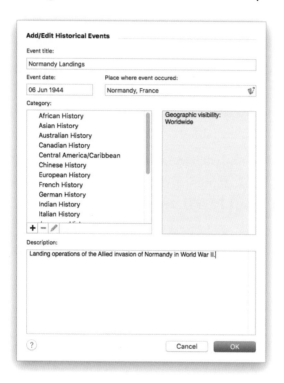

- **Event title.** Enter a short title for the event.

- **Event date.** Enter the date or date range of the event.

- **Place where event occurred.** Enter the location of the event.

- **Category.** Choose a historical category from the list or add your own categories. You can also edit and delete the default categories.

- **Description.** Enter a summary of the historical event.

5 Click **OK**.

Customising the Tree Tab Editing Panel

By default, these facts appear on the editing panel of the Tree tab in the People workspace: name, sex, birth date and place, death date and place, and marriage date and place. If you often include burials or christenings, you can add these facts to the editing panel so you can enter the information more easily.

1   Go to the **Tree** tab on the People workspace. The editing panel appears with its default facts.

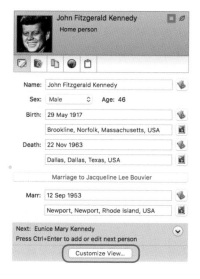

2   Click **Customize View**. The Customize View dialog opens.

3   In the Individual facts section or the Shared facts section, select a fact; then click the right arrow button to add the fact to the Selected facts sections.

4   To change the order in which the facts are displayed on the panel, select a fact and click the up or down arrows.

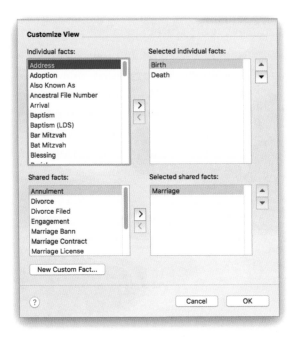

5   Click **OK**. The editing panel now includes the new fact.

Entering User Information

You can enter information that identifies you as the creator of your trees. This information is automatically added to your tree file if you export and send it to another family member or researcher.

1   Choose **Tools>User Information**. The User Information dialog opens.

2   Type your information and click **OK**.

Chapter Fourteen
Family Tree Problem Solver

No matter how organised you are or how carefully you enter data, errors can creep into your tree. Whether you've added a child to the wrong family or spelt your ancestor's name incorrectly, Family Tree Maker makes it easy to clean up your tree.

Straightening Out Relationships

At some point in your research you may discover that a certain individual doesn't belong in your tree and you need to delete him or her. Or maybe you added a child to the wrong family. Cleaning up relationship issues as soon as you find them prevents them from multiplying.

Merging Duplicate Individuals

After months and years of gathering names and dates, your family tree may become a bit disorderly. You might discover that Flossie and Florence are actually the same person. If you've entered duplicate individuals, you should merge them together (instead of deleting one) so that you don't lose any information.

Family Tree Maker can assess your tree and show you individuals who might be duplicates.

Note: Before you merge individuals, make a backup of your tree. If you need help see "Backing Up a Tree File" on page 223.

Finding Duplicate Individuals

After adding a lot of new information or merging a family member's tree with your own, it's a good idea to check for duplicate individuals.

1   Choose **Edit>Find Duplicate People**. The Find Duplicate List opens.

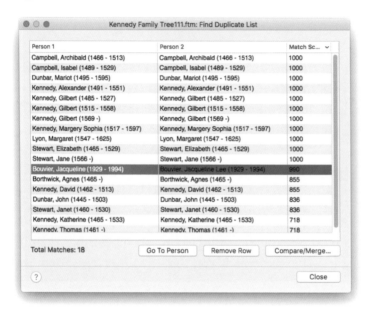

In the Person 1 and Person 2 columns you'll see the individuals who might be duplicates. (You can click the column header to sort a column alphabetically.) In the third column you'll see a match score—the higher the number, the more likely it is that the individuals are a match. A score of 1000 means the individuals are almost exact matches.

2   To merge a pair of individuals (or just compare the two), select a row and click **Compare/Merge**. The Individual Merge dialog opens. To complete the merge, continue from step 5 in the "Merging Individuals" section on page 268.

Merging Individuals

If you discover that two individuals in your tree are actually the same person, you can merge the two together and retain all the facts and sources associated with each person.

1 Go to the **Tree** tab on the People workspace and select one of the duplicate individuals in the Index.

2 Click the down arrow next to the **People** button on the main toolbar and choose **Merge Two Specific Individuals** from the pop-up menu. The Index of Individuals opens.

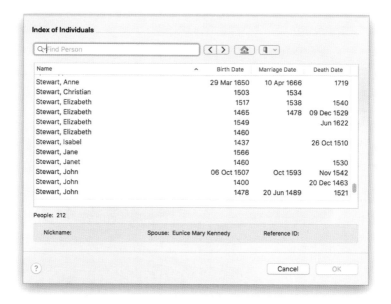

3 Select the name of the other duplicate individual. You can use the scroll bar to move up and down the list, or type a name (enter the last name first) in the search field.

4 Click **OK**. The Individual Merge dialog opens.

The two columns show the facts attached to each individual.

5   Use the buttons next to the facts to determine how each fact will
    be merged:

    •   To keep a fact and mark it as preferred, select the button next
        to the fact. The corresponding fact for the other individual
        will be merged as an alternate fact unless you discard it.

    •   To remove a fact, click the **Alternate** arrow and choose
        Discard from the pop-up menu. Although you can discard
        any fact you like, it is usually a good idea to keep all facts in
        case they turn out to be relevant. If you discard a fact, you can
        preserve its sources, media items, and notes by clicking the
        corresponding checkbox in the **Keep** group.

        Note: To learn more about preferred and alternate facts, see
        "Adding Alternate Facts" on page 45.

6   Click **OK** to complete the merge.

Removing an Individual from a Tree

If you've mistakenly added an individual who isn't related to you, don't worry. Family Tree Maker makes it easy to delete any individual and his or her information from your tree.

1   Go to the **Tree** tab on the People workspace.

2   In the Index or family group view, Control-click the individual you want to delete.

3   Choose **Delete Person** from the shortcut menu.
    All notes, tasks, and media links associated with the person will be permanently deleted.

> Note: Whenever you want to remove someone permanently from your tree, always use the Delete Person command. If you try to delete someone by removing his or her name from the Name fact, you won't actually delete the individual—or any of his or her facts or relationships.

Removing a Marriage

As you continue your research you might find that you've connected a couple incorrectly. In this case you'll need to delete any marriage facts you've entered and also detach the individuals from each other.

1   Go to the **Tree** tab on the People workspace and select the appropriate couple.

2   Click the **Person** tab for one of the individuals. Then click **Facts** to open the Individual & Shared Facts pane.

3   Control-click the **Marriage** fact and choose **Delete Fact** from the shortcut menu.

Note: If you don't delete the Marriage fact, the individual will
still be considered married to an unknown person.

4   To detach the individual from the current spouse, click the
down arrow next to the **People** button on the main toolbar and
choose **Attach/Detach Person>Detach Selected Person** from
the pop-up menu.

5   Select the checkbox for the incorrect spouse. If the couple has
children, you can select their checkboxes to detach them from
the selected individual too.

6   Click **Detach**.

Detaching a Child from the Wrong Parents

If you've added a child to the wrong parents, you can detach the
child from the family without deleting them from your tree.

1 Go to the **Tree** tab on the People workspace.

2 Make sure the correct family is the focus of the family group view.

3 Select the child.

Detach Living Shriver

Select any relationships from which you want to detach Living Shriver

Fathers
☑ Robert Sargent Shriver
Mothers
☐ Eunice Mary Kennedy

?   Cancel   Detach

4 Click the **People** button on the main toolbar and choose **Attach/Detach Person>Detach Selected Person** from the shortcut menu.

5 Select the checkboxes next to the father and/or mother.

6 Click **Detach**.

Attaching a Child to a Father and Mother

If you've added an individual and his or her parents to your tree, but you didn't know they were related when you entered them, you can still link them together.

1 Go to the **Tree** tab on the People workspace.

2 Make sure the individual you want to attach to his or her parents is the focus of the Index or family group view.

3 Click the **People** button on the main toolbar, click the down arrow next to the button, and choose **Attach/Detach Person>Attach Mother/Father** from the people menu.

4 Select the father or mother from the list and click **OK**. If the father or mother has multiple spouses, you'll need to choose which family the child belongs to.

5 Choose the appropriate family and click **Attach**.

Fixing Text Mistakes

It's easy to introduce errors into your tree. It can happen if you transcribed a record too quickly or imported incorrect notes from a family member's tree, for example. Family Tree Maker has several tools that can help you look for misspellings, inaccurate dates, and duplicate facts.

Global Spell Checker

The global spell checker lets you search for errors in your tree.

1 Choose **Tools>Global Spell Check**.

2 Change these options as necessary:

- **Fact descriptions.** Select this checkbox to check spelling in fact descriptions.

- **Notes.** Select this checkbox to check spelling in all notes.

- **Media.** Select this checkbox to check spelling in media captions and descriptions.

- **Tasks.** Select this checkbox to check spelling in all tasks in the research to-do list.

- **Sources.** Select this checkbox to search citation detail and citation text fields.

3 Click **Begin Checking**. If the spell checker finds a potential error, it displays the word in the "Not in dictionary" field.

4 Replace or ignore the word using the spell check buttons. When the spell check is complete. Click **Close**.

Find and Replace Tool

You may have mistakenly spelt an individual's name wrong throughout your tree or perhaps you abbreviated a place name that you want to spell out in full now. You can use Find and Replace to correct these mistakes—one by one or all at the same time.

1 Choose **Edit>Find and Replace**.

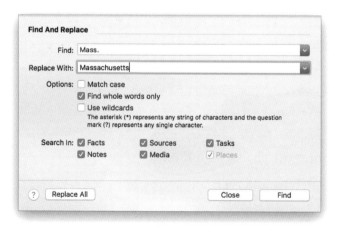

2 Type the term you want to search for in the **Find** field. Then type the new term you want to use in the **Replace With** field.

3 Select one or more of these options:

- To find words that match your search term exactly, including uppercase and lowercase letters, select the **Match case** checkbox.

- To find only entire words that match your search term, select the **Find whole words only** checkbox. (For example, a search for Will would not show results for William or Willton.)

- To search using wildcards, select the **Use wildcards** checkbox. Wildcards allow you to search for one or more missing characters. An asterisk (*) replaces multiple characters; a search for "Man*" could find Manchester, Mansfield, or Manhattan. A question mark (?) replaces one character; a search for Su?an would find Susan and Suzan.

4 Select the checkbox for each part of the tree you want to search. If you're not sure where the information is, you might want to select all the checkboxes.

5 Click **Find**. The first result that matches your search term appears.

6 If you want to replace the search term with the new term, click **Replace**.

Tip: You can also replace all matching search results by clicking the **Replace All** button. Before you do though, back up your tree file because you cannot undo these changes.

7 To find the next match, click **Find Next**.

8 Continue searching and replacing terms, as necessary. When you've finished, click **Close**.

Merging Duplicate Facts

If you have multiple versions of the same fact, you can merge them together. You can choose only one date and place for the fact. If you have multiple descriptions, they will be combined into one.

1   Go to the **Person** tab on the People workspace and select the appropriate individual.

2   Click **Facts**. Then Control-click one of the duplicate facts and select **Merge Duplicate Facts**.

3   Select the checkboxes next to the facts you want to merge and click **Next**.

4   Select the date and location you want to keep.

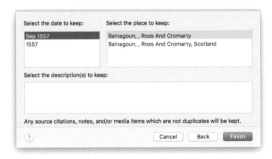

5   Click **Finish**.

Running the Data Errors Report

Family Tree Maker can search your tree and identify potential errors. For example, it can look for blank fields or date problems, such as an individual being born before his or her parents were born. It's a good idea to run the Data Errors Report every so often to make sure your tree is as error free as possible.

1   Go to the **Collection** tab on the Publish workspace. In **Publication Types**, select **Person Reports**.

2   Double-click the **Data Errors Report** or select the report icon and click the **Detail** tab.

3   To choose which errors the report will show, click the **Errors to include** button on the editing toolbar.

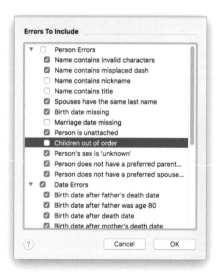

4   Select the checkboxes next to the errors you want to search for. Then click **OK**. The Data Errors Report opens.

5   To fix an error immediately, just click an individual's name in the report. An editing window will open.

Standardising Locations

When you import a tree or manually enter a location, Family Tree Maker checks the location against its database of three million places. If any misspellings are found, or if the place doesn't match any sites in the database, a location is considered "unidentified".

You should examine these "unidentified" locations occasionally and make any necessary changes. In some cases, you'll want to leave the name exactly as it is. For example, if a town or city no longer exists, or the county boundaries have changed over the years, you'll want to keep the location's name as it is. However, in most cases, you'll want to identify locations to keep your tree consistent and to make sure that locations are grouped together correctly on the Places workspace.

Identifying a Single Location

If you see a question mark icon next to a place name in your tree, you can try to identify the place in the locations database.

1   Click the **Places** button on the main toolbar.

2   Control-click the unidentified location (with a question mark icon) in the Places panel and choose **Resolve This Place Name**.

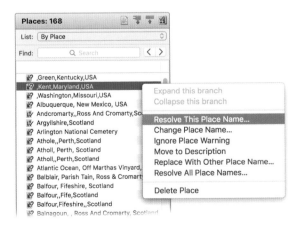

3 Do one of the following:

- If a suggestion matches the location in your tree, click its name in "Suggested place names" and click **Replace**.

- If no locations are a match, you can ignore part of a location by clicking the **Move first segment to place detail** arrow. When the updated location finally has a match, click **Replace**. (You can also click **Ignore** to leave the location as it is.)

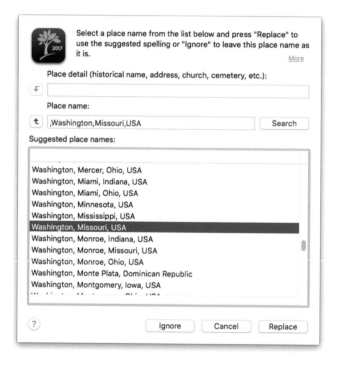

Note: Ignoring part of a location doesn't change how it is displayed in your tree; it simply allows the location to be grouped together correctly on the Places workspace.

Identifying Multiple Locations

If you've imported a tree or merged someone's tree into your own, you'll probably have many place names that don't match the other locations in your tree. Instead of updating each location one at a time, you can identify multiple locations at once.

1   Choose **Tools>Resolve All Place Names**.

2   To back up your tree file before you update your locations, click **Backup**. The Backup dialog opens. Change any options as necessary and click **Backup**.

The Resolve All Place Names dialog opens. Each unidentified location is listed, along with a suggested replacement location.

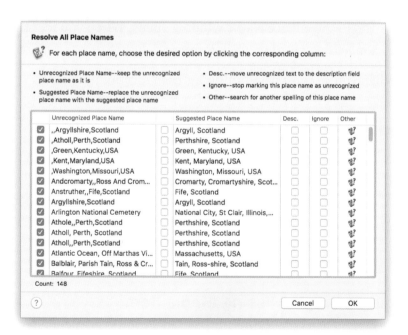

3 For each listed location, select the checkbox for the option
you want to use:

- **Unrecognized Place Name.** Select this checkbox to leave the
location as it is.

- **Suggested Place Name.** Select this checkbox to change the
current location to the suggested location.

- **Desc.** Select this checkbox to move the location's name from
the Place field to the Description field.

- **Ignore.** Click this checkbox to leave the location as it is. The
location name will no longer be "unidentified".

- **Other.** To see other locations that might match the current
place name, or to ignore only part of a location, click **Other**.
The Resolve Place Name window opens. When you identify
a matching location, click **Replace**.

4 When you've chosen an option for each location, click **OK**.

Finding Missing Media Items

If you move a media item from one folder to another on your
computer after you've added it to a tree, the link to your tree will be
broken and the item will be considered as "missing". You won't be
able to view, print, or export the item anymore until it is relinked
to your tree. You can search for missing media items to relink
individually or all at once.

Finding a Single Missing Media Item

On the Media workspace, the editing panel shows the media item's
name and location on your computer. If a media item is no longer
linked to your tree, you'll see a red "File not found" message. To
relink the media item, click the link and locate the item.

Finding All Missing Media Items

Family Tree Maker can search for all missing media items and help you relink them to your tree.

1 Click the **Media** button on the main toolbar. Then click the down arrow next to the button and choose **Find Missing Media** from the pop-up menu.

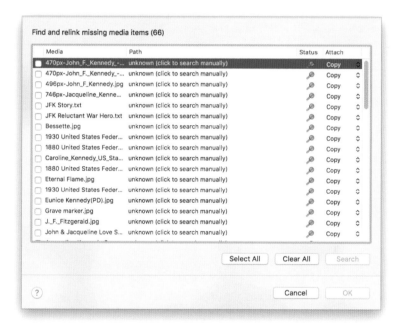

2 Select the checkboxes next to the items you want to locate or click **Select All** to find all broken media links.

3 Click **Search**. If Family Tree Maker finds the file, its current location is displayed in the Path column and a check mark (tick) appears in the Status column. If Family Tree Maker can't find the file, click its row in the Path column to search for it yourself.

4 When you've finished, click **OK**.

Troubleshooting

Although we hope you never have problems while using Family Tree Maker, all computers and software have their own incompatibilities. This chapter identifies several common problems and includes ways to fix them.

If you don't find an answer to your question, you can get help at support.familytreemaker.com. Type your issue in the search field and press **Return**.

When dealing with technical issues, you should make sure that your computer meets or exceeds the system requirements. Also, bear in mind that the more information you enter, the greater the amount of free hard disk space and available RAM you will need. If you are going to include a lot of pictures, audio, or video files in your trees, you will need a substantial amount of hard disk space.

Ancestry Issues

Because Family Tree Maker and Ancestry are closely linked together, you may encounter some website-related issues when using Family Tree Maker.

I am having trouble logging in to Ancestry.

Your computer may not be connected to the Internet. Make sure that you are able to access and sign in to Ancestry using a standard Web browser (*Safari*, etc.). If you are unable to access the website, you'll need to fix your Internet connection first.

Make sure Internet access is enabled in Family Tree Maker. To do this, go to the **File** menu and choose **Go Online**. (If the menu command "Go Offline" appears, Internet access is already enabled.)

Make sure that your computer's date and time are correctly set to your time zone. They can be adjusted by clicking on the date and time in the upper right-hand corner of your screen, then selecting "Open Date & Time Preferences…".

I have a problem getting Ancestry hints.

Make sure your FTM tree is uploaded and linked to the Ancestry tree.

Sign in to Ancestry using your usual Web browser and make sure there are hints in the Ancestry tree to which your FTM tree is linked.

Try closing and then opening your FTM tree.

When I try to access a record on Ancestry, I see an error message. What does it mean?

Occasionally you may come across one of these error messages:

> Document contains no data.

> 503 Service Unavailable.

> We're sorry, this page is temporarily unavailable.

These types of errors usually indicate a temporary issue with your Internet Service Provider (ISP) or the Ancestry website. To resolve the issue, refresh or reload the Web page by pressing **Command+Shift+R**. Or you can try to view the page again later.

If you keep seeing the same error message, you should clear your temporary Internet files in Safari (both cache and cookies).

I have problems printing and saving information I find on Ancestry when I access the website through Family Tree Maker.

The Web Search feature lets you add records from Ancestry and also navigate the entire website. However, some features on Ancestry work better when accessed through a standard Web browser rather than through the Family Tree Maker browser because of the latter's limited functionality. If you're having trouble using an Ancestry feature in Web Search, click the **Browser Options** button (to the left of the Address field) and choose "Open in New Window" to open the site in your usual Web browser.

FamilySync Issues

I get an error message when I try to sync my FTM and Ancestry trees.

Occasionally you may get an error message when you try to sync your linked trees. This can occur when your Internet connection is interrupted during the syncing process. You can try to fix your Internet connection before trying to sync your tree again. If you need more help to resolve a sync issue, read "Troubleshooting Sync" in the FTM Support Center.

(Go to support.familytreemaker.com and enter "troubleshooting sync" in the search field.)

Check your Internet connection. If you have a dial-up Internet connection, or you have disabled your broadband connection, establish your Internet connection before you open Family Tree Maker. Make sure you can go to other websites.

Make sure Internet access is enabled in Family Tree Maker. To do this, go to the **File** menu and choose **Go Online**. (If the menu command "Go Offline" appears, Internet access is already enabled.)

Generate and send a Sync Error Report. Sending a Sync Error Report (sometimes also called a "Sync Error Log") will help technical support determine exactly what is causing the issue you are experiencing when using FamilySync. The easiest way to generate and send a Sync Error Report is to use the **FamilySync Report** dialog. This will create a report and deliver it to the Family Tree Maker technical support team automatically. You can access the dialog in two ways:

- If an error occurs during syncing, the **FamilySync Report** dialog will open automatically.

- You can open the dialog at any time by choosing **Send Sync Error Report** from the **Help** menu.

I synced my trees and I can't see all the media items in my Ancestry tree. What happened?

When you sync your trees, the tree data is transferred immediately. Media items are processed separately in the background. Because of this it may take a while for all your images to appear in your Ancestry tree. You can track the progress of your media sync using the Media processing status bar on the main toolbar.

To improve your chances of trouble-free syncing, read "Best Practices for Syncing" in the FTM Support Center. (Go to support.familytreemaker.com and enter "best practices" in the search field.)

Relationship Mistakes and Unknown Spouses

You can easily fix an incorrect relationship by detaching an individual, then attaching them to the correct person in your tree. In the case of an unknown spouse, you would detach them from the person in your tree and their children, if any. For help, read "Fixing Relationship Mistakes" in the FTM Support Center. (Go to support.familytreemaker.com and enter "relationship mistakes" in the search field.)

Damaged or Corrupt Files

I don't have a backup of my tree and my tree file won't open. Is there anything I can do?

Files can be damaged by viruses, a merging of corrupt data, incorrect shut down of Family Tree Maker, and so on. If you don't have a backup of your tree, you can try to fix your current file. For help, read "Repairing a Tree File" in the FTM Support Center.

(Go to support.familytreemaker.com and enter "repair" in the search field.)

Installation Problems

For the vast majority of users, Family Tree Maker installs without any problems. However, if you are experiencing difficulties you should test the installation DVD on another computer to verify that the disc is undamaged. If it turns out to be damaged, contact technical support for assistance. If the DVD works on another computer, one of these topics may help you resolve the problem.

I can't get Family Tree Maker to install on my computer.

Occasionally Family Tree Maker won't install on a computer for unexpected reasons. For help troubleshooting this, read "Troubleshooting Installation" in the FTM Support Center. (Go to support.familytreemaker.com and enter "installation" in the search field.)

Nothing happens when I put the disc in the DVD drive.

There may be fingerprints, scratches, or dust on the DVD. Remove the DVD from the drive and gently wipe it with a clean towel. Do not wipe with a circular motion; wipe from the inside edge to the outside edge.

I installed the application but it won't open.

The administrator of your network or computer may be blocking your access to the application. Contact your administrator.

The application may be damaged. Try reinstalling the application.

How do I manually uninstall Family Tree Maker 2017?

For instructions on uninstalling Family Tree Maker, read "Uninstalling FTM" in the FTM Support Center.

(Go to support.familytreemaker.com and enter "uninstalling" in the search field.)

Internet Connection Problems

I get an error message that says, "You are not connected to the Internet or are behind a firewall."

This error occurs when your Internet connection is inactive, or when something is blocking Family Tree Maker from using your Internet connection.

Make sure Internet access is enabled in Family Tree Maker. To do this, go to the **File** menu and choose **Go Online**. (If the menu command "Go Offline" appears, Internet access is already enabled.)

Check your Internet connection. If you have a dial-up Internet connection, or you have disabled your broadband connection, establish your Internet connection before you open Family Tree Maker. Make sure you can go to other websites. If you are still unable to use Family Tree Maker online features, you can troubleshoot this issue. Read "Troubleshooting Connectivity Issues" in the FTM Support Center. (Go to support.familytreemaker.com and enter "connectivity" in the search field.)

Performance Issues

Family Tree Maker is running slowly. What can I do?

If Family Tree Maker is running more slowly than expected, here are a few steps you can take to improve the software's performance.

- Make sure your computer meets or exceeds the system requirements.

- Run the Compact File tool to reindex your tree file and remove unnecessary data. (For instructions, see "Compressing a Tree File" on page 225.)

- Check your tree for duplicate individuals or sources. Merge them as necessary.

- Work offline. Consider temporarily disabling Internet access in Family Tree Maker. To do this, go to the **File** menu and choose **Go Offline**.

- Turn off Ancestry and FamilySearch hints. To do this, go to the **Family Tree Maker 2017** menu and choose **Preferences**. In the General pane, deselect **Show hints from Ancestry** and **Show hints from FamilySearch**.

- Disable Fastfields. Disabling Fastfields in large databases can speed things up. To do this, go to the **Family Tree Maker 2017** menu and choose **Preferences**. In the General pane, deselect all the Fastfields checkboxes.

Printing Problems

Many printing problems are related to the specific printer you're using. Before you begin, make sure your printer is turned on and connected to the computer correctly. Also, make sure you have looked through any documentation that came with your printer. If you don't find your issue in the topics below, you may want to contact the technical support service of the printer's manufacturer.

I am unable to print in Family Tree Maker.

Try to print an image or document from another program. This will verify whether the printer is functioning properly or not. If you can print something using another program, it means the problem you are having may be result of a conflict with Family Tree Maker.

The most common cause of printing issues involves conflicts between the application and printer driver, which acts as a translator between the printer and the application. Make sure that the driver for your printer is up to date. Most manufacturers make these drivers available as free downloads from their websites.

My photos are not printing clearly.

Try changing the image to a different format before you import it. Family Tree Maker accepts a variety of common file formats.

The original image may be of poor quality. If you scanned the photograph, you may need to rescan it.

Family Tree Maker crashes when I print charts and reports.

Make sure that the driver for your printer is up to date. Most manufacturers make these drivers available as free downloads from their websites.

Program Unexpectedly Shuts Down

Family Tree Maker may shut down unexpectedly, and you may see an error message.

Family Tree Maker keeps crashing. What can I do?

If Family Tree Maker is crashing frequently, it could be due to system or program updates being needed, file corruption, or other causes. For help troubleshooting this issue, read "FTM 2017 Crashes or Closes Unexpectedly" in the FTM Support Center.

(Go to support.familytreemaker.com and enter "crashes" in the search field.)

Software Updates

How can I make sure I have the latest software updates?

From time to time, updates that fix bugs and add new features in Family Tree Maker are released. Make sure that Family Tree Maker is up to date by going to the **Family Tree Maker 2017** menu and choosing **Check for Updates**. A message tells you if you need to update the software.

You can also check for free updates at www.familytreemaker.com.

Glossary

Ahnentafel German for ancestor table. In addition to being a chart, it also refers to a genealogical numbering system.

ancestor A person you are descended from—parent, grandparent, great-grandparent, etc.

Ancestry Hint The green leaf indicating that a person might have matching records on Ancestry.

Ancestry Member Tree (AMT) Same as Ancestry tree.

Ancestry tree An online family tree you have created on or uploaded to Ancestry.

blended family A family composed of a couple and their children from previous relationships and/or marriages, as well as any children they have together.

combined family view An option in the family group view that lets you view blended families.

CSV Comma Separated Values. A file format that organises information into fields and can be imported into a spreadsheet.

descendant A person who is descended from you—your child, grandchild, great-grandchild, etc.

editing panel   A section of a workspace that lets you easily edit and view information for a specific individual or item.

export   To transfer data from one computer to another or from one computer application to another.

family group sheet   A chart or report that displays information about a single family—father, mother, and children.

family group view   Shows a single family—father, mother, and their children—in Family Tree Maker.

family view   One of the display options for the tree viewer on the People workspace. Similar to the vertical pedigree chart.

FamilySearch hint   The blue square indicating that a person might have matching records on FamilySearch.org.

FamilySync   A feature that lets you link trees from Family Tree Maker and Ancestry so that changes made to an FTM tree will be reflected in the Ancestry tree and vice versa.

Fastfields   A feature that reminds you of locations and people you've entered previously so that when you type a new place or name, you'll see possible matches.

FTM tree   A family tree you have created in or downloaded to Family Tree Maker.

GEDCOM   GEnealogical Data COMmunication. A standard designed by the Family History Department of The Church of Jesus Christ of Latter-day Saints for transferring data between different genealogy software applications.

genealogy report   A narrative-style report that details a family through one or more generations and includes basic facts about each member.

generation   The period of time between the birth of one group of individuals and the next—usually twenty-five to thirty years.

given name   The first (and middle) name given to a child at birth or at his or her birth. Also known as a Christian name.

hint   See Ancestry Hint and FamilySearch hint.

home person   The main individual in your tree.

HTML   HyperText Markup Language. The standard language for creating and formatting Web pages.

icon   A small picture or symbol that represents a program, file, or folder on your computer. Double-clicking an icon causes the application to run, the folder to open, or the file to be displayed.

import   To bring a file into an application. The file may have been created in the same or a different application.

maternal ancestor   An ancestor on the mother's side of the family.

media item   Photographs, scanned documents, audio files, or videos that you can add to a tree.

paternal ancestor   An ancestor on the father's side of the family.

PDF   Portable Document Format. A file format that retains printer formatting so that when it is opened it looks as it would on the printed page.

pedigree chart   A chart that shows the direct ancestors of an individual. Also known as an ancestor tree.

pedigree view   One of the display options for the tree viewer on the People workspace. Similar to the standard pedigree chart.

preferred   A term Family Tree Maker uses in reference to parents, spouses, or duplicate events indicating that you want to see the preferred selection first or have it displayed in charts and reports.

primary person   The individual who is currently the focus of the workspace, chart, or report.

RTF   Rich Text Format. A basic text file format that can be opened in almost all word-processing programs.

siblings   Children of the same parents.

Soundex   A system that assigns a code to a surname based on how it sounds rather than how it is spelt.

source   A place where you found specific information, such as a historical records, a book, or an interview.

source citation   The individual details about where information is located within a source.

surname   The family name or last name of an individual.

Web clipping   The ability to "clip" text or images from a Web page and add them elsewhere, like to your Family Tree Maker tree.

Web Dashboard   A feature on the Plan workspace that lets you view your Ancestry account and trees.

Web Merge   A feature that lets you take records you've found on Ancestry and FamilySearch and add them to your Family Tree Maker tree.

workspace   A major grouping of Family Tree Maker features. Each workspace can be opened from the main toolbar.

Index

A

addresses, entering, 43
adoptions, indicating, 58
aerial maps, 109
Ahnentafels, 173–174
AKA (Also Known As) names
    entering, 43
AKA names, including in Index,
   254–255
alerts, preferences for, 256–257
alternate facts, entering, 45
ancestor reports, 182
ancestors
    reports of, 182
Ancestry
    error messages on, 285
    hints from, 121–123
    records on, 125
    searching, 124–127
    searching automatically, 252
    search results, merging into
        trees, 130–134
    search tips, 128, 129
Ancestry Hints
    ignoring, 123
    turning on, 252
    viewing, 122

    viewing ignored hints, 124
Ancestry Member Trees. See trees
   (Ancestry)
Ancestry trees
    comparison with FTM trees,
        228–230
    inviting others to view,
        237–238
    privacy options, 227
Ancestry Web Dashboard, 11
anniversary lists, 177
annotated bibliographies, 186
audio files. See media items

B

backgrounds
    for charts, 157–158
    for reports, 193
backups
    automatic, preferences for, 251
    creating, 223–225
    restoring files from, 224
bibliographies, 186
biographies, creating with Smart
   Stories, 63–64
bird's-eye-view maps, 110

birth dates
    calculating, 243
    entering, 35
birthday lists, 177
birth order, sorting children by, 246
birthplaces, entering, 35
blended families, viewing, 53–54
book-building tool
    overview, 201
Bookmarks button, 13
books
    chapters in, reordering, 212
    charts, adding, 208
    creating new, 201–202
    exporting as PDF, 213
    footers, changing, 202–203
    headers, changing, 202–203
    images, adding, 206–207
    index of individuals, adding,
        210
    place holders, adding, 208–209
    printing, 213
    reports, adding, 208
    saved, accessing, 202
    table of contents, adding, 209
    text item
        adding manually, 203–205
        importing, 205–206
    titles, adding, 202–203
borders, adding to charts, 166–168
bow tie charts, 151
boxes, adding to charts, 166–168

C

calculators
    for dates, 243
    for relationships, 242–243

Soundex, 241
calendars, 188
call numbers, 76
captions, entering for media items,
    93
categories
    for media items, 102
    for to-do lists, creating,
        248–249
causes of death, entering, 43
cemeteries, locating on maps, 113
censuses available on Ancestry, 125
charts
    adding photographs to,
        157–159
    adding to books, 208
    backgrounds for, 157–158
    borders for, 166–168
    bow tie, 151
    boxes for, 166–168
    centring on pages, 164
    choosing facts to include,
        154–156
    creating, 154
    about descendants, 150
    displaying everyone in tree,
        152–153
    display names for locations
        entering, 120
    emailing, 172
    family group sheets, 180–181
    family tree, 151
    fan, 152
    fonts for, changing, 168
    footers for, changing, 162–163
    headers for, changing, 162–163
    hourglass
        horizontal, 149

standard, 147–149
including sources in, 157
pedigree
    standard, 146
    vertical, 146
photographs of individuals in,
    assigning, 95–96
printing, 171
about relationships, 153
saving
    in Family Tree Maker,
        170–171
    as files, 170–171
spacing of columns, changing,
    163–164
titles for, 156
children
    adding to trees, 39–40
    adopted, indicating, 58
    attaching to parents, 271–272
    detaching from parents,
        270–271
    foster, indicating, 58
    natural, indicating, 58
    order for, changing, 40
christenings, entering, 43
churches, locating on maps, 113
Citation detail field, 77
citations. See source citations
Citation text field, 77
Collection tab (Publish), 21
colour coding, 50
combined family view, 53–54
Compact File tool, 225–226
Companion Guide (PDF), 6
connection error messages, 289
contact lists, 177
contributors in Ancestry trees, 239

Convert Names tool, 244
courthouses, locating on maps, 113
CSV format, saving reports in,
    197–198
custom facts
    creating, 258–259
    sentences for, modifying, 260
custom reports, 175
custom templates (for charts)
    creating, 169
    using, 169

D

Data Errors Report, 276
Data Errors Reports, 175–176
Date Calculator, 243
dates
    of births, entering, 35
    calculating, 243
    errors for, 256–257
    guidelines for entering, 36
    inaccurate, locating, 276
    preferences for, 255–256
deleting individuals from tree, 269
descendant reports, 174, 182
descendants
    charts displaying, 150
    reports of, 174, 182
Detail tab (Media), 19
Detail tab (Publish), 21
disclaimer, legal, 283
divorces, indicating, 58
Documented Facts Reports, 187
double dates, preferences for, 256
downloading
    Ancestry trees, 26–29

duplicate individuals
    finding, 266
    merging, 267–268
DVDs, troubleshooting installa-
    tion, 288

E

editing panel (Family tab)
    customising fields on, 263–264
    customising tabs on, 253
editing panel (People workspace)
    overview, 16
editing photos, 96
editors in Ancestry trees, 239
emailing
    charts, 172
    reports, 199–200
emigration information, entering,
    43
error messages
    on Ancestry, 285
errors
    creating reports of, 175–176,
        276
    data entry, 272–276
    File Not Found (media items),
        280
    finding and replacing, 273–274
    installation, troubleshooting,
        288–289
    missing media items, 280–281
    preferences for alerts, 256–257
    for unidentified locations
        resolving, 277–280
        setting up, 257
    for unlikely dates, 256–257

Unrecognized Place Name,
    277–280
events. See facts
exporting
    books, 213
    trees, 220–221
extended family charts, 152–153

F

facts
    adding sources for, 71–76
    alternate, 45
    associated with locations, view-
        ing, 115–116
    copying and pasting, 44
    custom, creating, 258–259
    duplicate, merging, 275
    entering, 41–43
    including in charts, 154–156
    including in reports, 189–192
    making private, 46
    media items for, adding, 90–92
    online, saving to trees, 135–136
    predefined, modifying,
        260–261
    preferred, 45–46
    sentences for, modifying, 260
    source citations, creating for,
        77–80
    sourced, reports of, 187
    transferring between Family
        Tree Maker and Ancestry,
        228
    using in Smart Stories, 63
families
    blended, viewing, 53–54
    combined, viewing, 53–54

locations associated with, 118
    step, viewing, 53–54
family group sheets, 180–181
family group view
    displaying blended families,
        53–54
    overview, 16
    sorting children in, 40
FamilySearch
    hints, 122
    searching, 130
FamilySearch hints of matches
    turning off and on, 252
FamilySync
    comparison between Ancestry
        and FTM trees, 228–229
    conflicts between trees, resolv-
        ing, 234–235
    downloading Ancestry trees,
        27–28
    log of changes, 231–233
    options for, 230
    privacy for linked trees, chang-
        ing, 236–237
    status of linked trees, 232
    syncing trees manually, 233
    unlinking trees, 236
    uploading trees to Ancestry,
        226–228
family tree charts, 151
family view, 15
fan charts, 152
Fastfields, 253–254
favourite websites
    adding to, 141
    sorting, 142
feedback, providing, 7

file names
    for media items, changing, 100
File Not Found errors (media
    items), 280
files
    backing up, 223–224
    compressing, 225–226
    damaged, troubleshooting,
        288–289
    exporting, 220–221
    importing, 24–25
    media items, missing, 280–281
    restoring from backups, 224
file sizes
    reducing, 225–226
    viewing, 218
filtered lists
    managing saved, 14
    opening, 13
    saving, 13
Find and Replace tool, 273–274
Find Individual tool, 244–245
fonts
    changing in charts, 168
    changing in reports, 195
    in books, changing, 206
footers
    for books, 202–203, 211–212
    for charts, 162–163
    for reports, 194
foster children, indicating, 58

G

GEDCOMs
    importing, 24–25
    saving trees as, 220–222

GPS (Global Positioning System) coordinates
   entering, 119
Gregorian calendar, 256
guests in Ancestry trees, 239
guide, organisation of, xix

H

headers
   for books, 202–203, 211–212
   for charts, 162–163
   for reports, 194
Help
   Companion Guide (PDF), 6
   Help Tags, 6
   onscreen, 5–6
   technical support, contacting, 7
Help Tags, 6
hierarchy list, for groups, 115–116
hints. See Ancestry Hints
historical events for timelines,
   creating or editing, 261–262
History button, 13
home person, 13, 30–31
horizontal hourglass charts, 149
hospitals, locating on map, 113
hourglass charts
   horizontal, 149
   standard, 147–149
HTML, saving reports as, 197–198

I

ID numbers, 245–246
images. See media items,See
   also media items; photographs

immigration information, entering,
   43
importing
   trees, 24–25
Index
   including
      married names, 254–255
      titles, 254–255
indexes, adding to books, 210
index of individuals
   including in books, 210
   reports of, 177
Index of Individuals Reports, 177
individuals
   adding media items for, 90–92
   addresses, entering, 43
   basic information for, entering,
      35–41
   causes of death, entering, 43
   christenings, entering, 43
   default photo for, assigning,
      95–96
   duplicate
      finding, 266
      merging, 267–268
   emigration information, enter-
      ing, 43
   finding specific people,
      244–245
   immigration information,
      entering, 43
   locations associated with,
      117–118
   marriage of, entering, 38
   media items for, choosing sort
      order, 100
   physical descriptions, enter-
      ing, 43

reference numbers for, 245–246
removing marriages, 269–270
reports about, 176
slide show of media items,
    103–106
installation
    automatic, 4
    registering software, 4
    system requirements, 3
    troubleshooting, 288–289
Internet connections, error mes-
    sages for, 289

J

Julian calendar, 256

K

keyboard shortcuts, 10
Kinship Reports, 181

L

layout
    poster, 164
layout, changing for charts,
    163–164
LDS interface options, displaying,
    251
LDS Ordinances Reports, 176
LDS Ordinance Summary Reports,
    177
legal disclaimer, 283
libraries, locating on maps, 113
linked trees
    comparison between Ancestry
        and FTM trees, 228–230

conflicts between, 234–236
inviting others to view,
    237–238
log of changes, 231–233
multiple FTM trees to Ances-
    try, 229
privacy for, changing, 236–237
status of, 232
syncing manually, 233
syncing options, 230–231
troubleshooting, 286–287
unlinking, 236
uploading to Ancestry, 226–227
locations
    associated with families,
        118–119
    associated with individuals,
        117–118
    completing with Fastfields, 253
    display name for, 120
    entering, 36
    facts associated with, 116–117
    finding nearby places of inter-
        est, 113–115
    GPS coordinates for, entering,
        119
    guidelines for entering, 37
    reports of usage, 184
    standardising, preference for,
        251
    transferring between Family
        Tree Maker and Ancestry,
        229
    troubleshooting, 277–280
    unidentified
        resolving multiple, 279–280
        resolving one at a time,
            277–278

warnings for, 257
viewing for individuals,
    117–118
viewing in groups, 115
log of sync changes, 231–233

M

main toolbar, 10
maps
    GPS coordinates for locations,
        entering, 119
    printing, 114
maps (Microsoft Bing Maps)
    aerial, 109
    bird's-eye, 110
    road, 110
    viewing, 107–111
    zooming in and out of,
        111–112
Marriage Reports, 181
marriages
    entering, 38
    multiple, 55–57
    removing from individuals,
        269–270
    reports of, 181
    statuses of, 58
married names
    including in Index, 254–255
media categories, creating, 102
Media Item Reports, 185
media items
    adding
        for facts, 90–92
    adding to Smart Stories, 66
    categories for, 102
    choosing sort order, 100

display of, changing, 92–93
editing within Family Tree
    Maker, 100
entering details about, 93–94
file names, changing, 100
linking to
    source citations, 81
linking to individuals, 98–99
missing, troubleshooting,
    280–281
notes for, 94
online, adding to trees,
    137–138
printing, 106
printing, troubleshooting, 291
privacy for, 93
reports about, 184–186
scanning into Family Tree
    Maker, 91–92
slide show of, 103–106
Smart Stories, 60–66
transferring between Family
    Tree Maker and Ancestry,
    228
types of, 89
Media Usage Reports, 186
Media workspace, 19
medical conditions, entering, 43
menus, 10
merging
    Ancestry records into trees,
        130–134
    duplicate facts, 275
    duplicate individuals, 267–269
migration paths
    maps of, 117–119
    printing, 114

N

names
  completing with Fastfields, 253–254
  guidelines for entering, 39
  including AKA names in Index, 254–256
  including married names in Index, 254–256
  nicknames, entering, 43
  standardising tool, 244
  titles in, 43
nicknames, entering, 43
notes
  adding for individuals, 47–48
  create using online information, 138–139
  display size, changing, 48
  for media items, 94
  personal, 47
  printing, 49
  privacy for, 48
  reports of, 178
  research, 48
  for source citations, 82–83
  spell checking, 272–273
  transferring between Family Tree Maker and Ancestry, 228–229
  using in Smart Stories, 66
Notes Reports, 178

O

online facts, adding to trees, 135–136

online images, adding to trees, 137–138
Outline Ancestor Reports, 182

P

page numbers
  for books, 202–203
  including in charts, 162
  including in reports, 194
parents
  adding to trees, 40–41
  attaching children to, 271–272
  detaching children from, 270–271
  reports about, 183
partner relationships, indicating, 57
PDFs
  of charts, creating, 170–171
  Companion Guide, accessing, 6
  of books, creating, 213
  of reports, creating, 197–198
pedigree charts
  standard, 146
  vertical, 146–147
pedigree view, 15
People workspace, 12–16
performance issues, troubleshooting, 290
personal notes, 47
Person tab, 17
photo albums, 184
Photo Darkroom, 96
photographs. See media items,See also media items
  adding to books, 206–207
  assigning default for individuals, 95–96

available on Ancestry, 125
for charts, 157–159
missing, troubleshooting,
    280–281
printing, 106
scanning into Family Tree
    Maker, 91–92
physical descriptions, entering, 43
place holders, adding to books,
  208–209
places. See locations
Places workspace, 18
Place Usage Reports, 184
Plan workspace, 10–11
portraits
    assigning to individuals, 95–96
    cropping in workspaces, 251
    defaults for charts, 95–96
    including in charts, 159–161
poster layout, 164
predefined facts
    modifying, 260–261
preferences
    for alerts, 256–257
    for automatic backups, 251
    for dates, 255–256
    for errors, 256–257
    for Fastfields, 253
    general, 250–251
    for names, 254–255
    for online searching, 252
    for tab displays, 253
preferred spouses, 55–56
preferred facts, 45–46
printing
    charts, 171
    large charts, 171
    maps, 114

media items, 106
notes for individuals, 49
reports, 198
troubleshooting, 285, 291–292
privacy
    for Ancestry trees, 227
    for Family Tree Maker trees,
    219
    for linked trees, changing,
        236–237
    for media items, 93
    for notes, 48
    roles in Ancestry trees, 239
problem solver. See errors; trouble-
    shooting
public trees, 227
Publish workspace, 21

R

reference notes, 78
reference numbers, automatic,
    245–246
registering software, 4
Register reports, 174
Relationship calculator, 242–243
relationships
    charts about, 153
    between children and parents,
        58
    between couples, 57
    details about, entering, 38
    media items for, adding, 38
    reference numbers for, 245–246
    removing marriages, 269–270
    reports about, 180–183
    status of, 58
    troubleshooting, 265–272

viewing for individuals, 54
removing individuals from tree, 269
reports
    adding to books, 208
    Ahnentafels, 173–174
    of ancestors, 173–174
    of anniversaries, 177
    of birthdays, 177
    choosing facts to include,
        189–192
    choosing individuals to in-
        clude, 192
    of contacts, 177
    creating, 189
    custom, 175
    customising, 189–195
    default settings for, changing,
        196
    of descendants, 174, 182
    display names for locations
        entering, 120
    of documented facts, 187
    emailing, 199–200
    of errors, 175–176, 276
    fact sentences for, 260
    fonts for, changing, 195
    about individuals, 176
    about kinship, 181
    about LDS Ordinances, 176,
        177
    about locations, 184
    about marriages, 181
    about media items, 185–186
    of notes, 178
    about parentage, 183
    printing, 198
    Register, 174
    about relationships, 180–183

    of research tasks, 179
    saving, 196–198
    of sources, 186–188
    of surnames, 178
    titles for, 193
repositories, 76, 83
    adding, 83
    editing, 86
    replacing, 85
    reviewing usage of, 84
requirements, system, 3
research notes, 48
roles in Ancestry trees, 237–238
RTF (Rich Text Format), saving
    reports in, 197–198

S

saving
    charts, 170–172
    reports, 196–200
scanning photograph into Family
    Tree Maker, 91–92
searching
    Ancestry, 124–127
    FamilySearch, 130
    online with Family Tree Maker,
        134
    for specific people, 244–245
search tips
    for Ancestry, 128
    for FamilySearch, 129
sentences for facts, modifying, 260
separations (marriage), indicating,
    58
settings, default
    changing for reports, 196
sharing trees

online, 237–238
slide show, creating, 103–106
Smart Stories
    adding facts, 63
    adding images, 66–67
    adding notes, 66
    adding sources, 65
    creating biographies with,
        63–64
    creating timelines with, 67
    overview, 60–61
    text, editing, 67–68
software updates
    Family Tree Maker, 292
sorting children by birth order, 246
Soundex calculator, 241
soundtracks, adding to slide shows,
    105
source citations
    adding notes about, 82–83
    attaching media items to, 81
    copying, 80
    explanation of, 69–70
    using multiple times, 78–80
sources
    adding, 71–72
    basic format, 75–76
    including in charts, 157
    overview, 69–70
    reports of, 186–188
    repositories for, 76
    spell checking, 272–273
    templates for, 72–74
    transferring between Family
        Tree Maker and Ancestry,
        229
    using in Smart Stories, 65
Sources workspace, 20

source templates, 72–75
Source Usage Reports, 188
spell checker
    using, 272–273
spouses
    adding to tree, 37–38
    adding to trees, 37–38
    multiple, 55–57
    preferred, 55–56
    switching between, 57
    unknown, 287
standard hourglass charts, 147–149
status (sync), viewing, 232
stepfamilies, viewing, 53–54
stories, transferring between Family
    Tree Maker and Ancestry, 229
support, contacting, 7
Surname Reports, 178
Sync Weather Report, 233
system defaults
    location for trees, 251
system requirements, 3

T

table of contents, creating for
    books, 209
tabs
    Collection (Publish), 21
    Current Tree, 10–11
    Detail (Media), 19
    Detail (Publish), 21
    displaying on editing panel, 253
    New Tree, 11
    Person, 17
task lists, 179
technical support, 7

templates (chart)
    creating, 169
    preferred, 169
    using, 169
templates (source), 72–75
text
    adding to books, 203–205
    finding and replacing, 273–274
    formatting in books, 206
    including in charts, 161
    online, adding to notes,
        138–139
    Smart Stories, editing, 67–68
    spell checking, 272–273
timelines
    creating in Smart Stories, 67
    historical events for, creating or
        editing, 261–262
    viewing, 59–60
titles
    changing for books, 202–204
    changing for charts, 156
    changing for reports, 193
    including in Index, 254–255
titles (in names)
    fact for, 43
to-do lists, 247–250
toolbars, 10
tools
    book-building, 201
    Compact File, 225–226
    Convert Names, 244
    Date Calculator, 243
    Find and Replace, 273–274
    Find Individual, 244–245
    Finding Duplicate People, 266
    managing historical events,
        261–262

Relationship calculator,
    242–243
Soundex calculator, 241
Web clipping, 135–140
Tooltips. See Help Tags
tree charts. See charts
trees
    backing up files, 223–225
    default directory for, 251
    deleting, 219
    exporting, 220–222
    number of generations in,
        viewing, 218
    number of individuals in, view-
        ing, 218
    opening, 217–218
    removing individual from, 269
    renaming, 218
    securing, 219
    size of file, reducing, 225–226
    statistics about, 218
trees (Ancestry)
    downloading, 26–29
    inviting others to view,
        237–238
trees (Family Tree Maker)
    adding
        children, 39–40
        notes, 47–48
        parents, 40–41
        spouses, 37–38, 55–56
    comparison with Ancestry
        trees, 228–230
    creating, 23–29
    guidelines for creating, 26
    home person of, 13, 30–31
    importing, 24–25

linking multiple FTM trees to
   Ancestry, 229
uploading and linking to Ancestry, 226–228
Tree tab
   customising fields on editing
      panel, 263–264
   family group view on, 16
   Index on, 12
   tree viewer on, 15
tree viewer, 15
   background colour, 16
troubleshooting
   accessing onscreen help, 5–6
   conflicts between linked trees,
      234–235
   contacting technical support, 7
   damaged files, 288–289
   data entry errors, 272–276
   Data Errors report, 276
   Data Errors Reports, 175–176
   FamilySync issues, 286–287
   installation, 288–289
   Internet connections, 289
   legal disclaimer, 283
   linked trees, 286–287
   marriages, removing, 269–270
   missing media items, 280–281
   performance issues, 290
   printing, 291–292
   program shuts down, 292
   reducing file size, 225–226
   relationships issues, 265–272
   software updates, 292
   unidentified locations, 277–280
   uninstalling Family Tree
      Maker, 289

U

uninstalling Family Tree Maker,
   289
unlinking trees, 236
unmarried couples, indicating, 57
Unrecognized Place Name error,
   277
unrelated individuals, adding to
   trees, 59
updates, software
   Family Tree Maker, 292
uploading
   trees to Ancestry, 225–229
user information, entering, 264

V

vertical pedigree charts, 146–147
videos. See media items

W

Web clipping tool, 135–140
Web links, adding for an individual,
   49
Web Merge Wizard, 130–134
Web pages. See also websites
Web pages, archiving, 140
Web Search
   merging result into trees,
      130–134
   preferences for, 252
   results, ignoring, 123
Web Search workspace, 22
websites
   archiving specific pages, 140

favourites
    adding to, 141
    sorting, 142
searching with Family Tree
    Maker, 134
for sources, 77
wildcards
    in Ancestry searches, 128
workspaces
    Media, 19
    People, 12–16
    Places, 18
    Plan, 10–11
    Publish, 21
    Sources, 20
    Web Search, 22

About the Original Author

Tana L. Pedersen

Tana has been writing and editing in the technology industry for more than fifteen years. She has earned several awards for her writing, including the Distinguished Technical Communication award from the Society for Technical Communication. Tana is author of *Beyond the Basics: A Guide for Advanced Users of Family Tree Maker 2012*, five editions of *The Official Guide to Family Tree Maker*, and co-author of *The Official Guide to RootsWeb.com*.